GOOD
HOUSEKEEPING
Chocolates, Sweets and Toffees

GOOD HOUSEKEEPING
Chocolates, Sweets and Toffees

by Good Housekeeping Institute

published in collaboration with
Tate & Lyle Refineries Limited

BOOK CLUB ASSOCIATES
LONDON

This edition published 1979 by
Book Club Associates
by arrangement with Ebury Press

Editor Patricia Mackinnon
Designer Derek Morrison
Colour photography by Paul Kemp
Line drawings by Hilary Evans

Jacket illustration shows:

Front (from the outside in)
Caramelled grapes (page 60), Chocolate dipped fondants (page
103), Chocolate rum truffles (page 107), Mocha truffles, Parisian
truffles (page 108)
Chocolate dipped fondants and caramels (page 103), Coconut ice
bars (page 53), Nut and cherry fudge (page 77)
Marzipan cherries, Neapolitan slices (page 32), Marzipan triangles
(page 33)
Fresh fruit jellies (page 36)
Caramelled strawberry (page 60)
Ginger fudge (page 71), bottom right

Back
Same sweets as front except for
Almond star (page 62) on top spoon

Filmset and printed in Great Britain by
BAS Printers Limited, Over Wallop, Hampshire
and bound by
Cambridge University Press, Cambridge

Contents

Introduction

Making 'homemade' sweets is an absorbing and rewarding hobby and with a little practice very professional results can be obtained.

Today most confectioners only sell pre-wrapped bars or boxes of sweets or chocolates and many old-fashioned favourites have disappeared completely. If you have nostalgic memories of sweets you used to eat as a child and now never see, or if you can find them but they don't taste the same, you may like to try your hand at making them. Most of them can easily be made at home and don't require complicated equipment or unusual ingredients.

The recipes in this book range from very simple uncooked mixtures to more ambitious sweets like nougat, treacle toffee and butterscotch that need greater skill and accuracy for a perfect finish. Everybody can have a go at sweet making regardless of their ability.

The uncooked sweets are perfect for beginners and particularly good for children as there is no heat involved. Great fun can be had by experimenting with colours and shapes of simple mixtures such as uncooked fondants, fudges and marzipans, and the results are edible! It is the perfect pastime for a wet Sunday afternoon.

Cooked sweets require more care to produce perfect results, but by following the recipes carefully, testing frequently and being accurate with temperatures, success can be guaranteed.

As well as the fact that there is so much fun to be had in making sweets, it is immensely satisfying being able to give away or raise funds from the products of your own kitchen. Homemade sweets and chocolates make the best of birthday and Christmas presents for people of all ages, and they are often the most sought after items on the stalls at fund raising occasions such as church or school fêtes, bazaars or bring and buy sales. If you become reasonably proficient at it, and can find a suitable outlet for your produce, sweet making can be a profitable occupation if you're housebound for any reason. And whether making sweets to give away or sell, the finishing touches make all the difference. Imaginative presentation need not be at all expensive, and we give plenty of ideas on how to pack and wrap the sweets you have made in the final chapter of this book.

What You Need – and What You Should Know

Equipment, Ingredients, Sugar boiling temperatures

EQUIPMENT

For simple sweet making it is not necessary to purchase any special equipment; most utensils can be found in any kitchen. If you intend making sweets regularly, however, or want to try some of the more involved recipes, it will be worth buying some of the items listed under 'Special Equipment' opposite.

Basics

Saucepans Large, strong, thick-based saucepans are essential to prevent burning or sticking. They should be deep rather than wide to avoid evaporation and to ensure that the bulb of the sugar thermometer, if one is used, is completely covered. The best pans are stainless steel, copper, brass or thick aluminium. Enamel and non-stick pans are not suitable as they will not stand up to high sugar boiling temperatures. Pans with a slightly rounded bottom are ideal and can be purchased from specialist suppliers (see page 125).

Tins The most useful tins for sweet making are square or rectangular straight-sided tins measuring about 18–20 cm (7–8 in) with a depth of about 2.5 cm (1 in), but obviously the size required will vary according to the quantity of mixture and we give details in each recipe. Non-stick tins are the best to use as they do not need such thorough greasing.

Spatulas A wooden spatula is useful for working fondants. Long handled spatulas ensure that the hands are well away from hot mixtures.

Palette knife A flexible stainless steel palette knife is more suitable than a spatula for turning toffees. It is also useful for shaping and can be used to lift and place sweets for drying.

Sugar boiling thermometer Perhaps this should come under the 'Special Equipment' category (see opposite), but for guaranteed results, a sugar thermometer really is recommended. The best thermometers are easy to read and well-graduated, with temperatures ranging from 16°C (60°F) to 182°C (360°F). They have a handle that can be of brass or wood and a sliding clip that will fit over the side of the

10

pan. For sugar boiling temperatures see page 14. To prepare a thermometer for use it should be seasoned by placing it in a pan of cold water, allowing the water to come to the boil and then leaving it in the water to cool.

When required, the thermometer should be placed in the syrup with the mixture covering the bulb. (This is most important if an accurate reading is to be taken.) It should be clipped over the side of the pan and allowed to stand upright, and the reading should be taken at eye level. If the mixture is being boiled for some time, make sure it doesn't set around the bulb, causing an inaccurate reading.

Clean the thermometer carefully after use as any sugar crystals stuck to it might spoil the next batch and prevent an accurate reading. Soak it in hot water until all the syrup has dissolved and dry very carefully before storing.

Scissors Very strong kitchen scissors are useful for cutting toffee, nougat, or jellies.

Cutters Various small shapes are useful for cutting fondants, marzipans, and other soft mixtures.

Special Equipment

Working surfaces A marble slab gives the best results for turning toffees and other boiled mixtures, but is rather expensive to buy. If you plan a lot of sweet making, however, it is worth spending time trying to obtain one. Old marble-topped tables or washstands can be purchased from junk shops and you can have your slab cut to size by a stonemason. Enamelled surfaces also produce good results and you can even use a heavy wooden chopping board as long as you grease it thoroughly before you begin. Laminated surfaces may be used only if they are able to withstand temperatures of up to 138°C (280°F).

Dipping forks These are the small forks used to dip sweets into chocolate or fondant mixtures. They may be looped or two-to-three-pronged. It is a good idea to have one of each as they may be used to give a variety of pattern and design on top of the finished sweet.

Patterns can be marked on top of the chocolates in the form of loops or raised designs, or even, with a little practice, by swirling a finger over the surface.

Cream rings Small metal rings are sometimes used for moulding peppermint creams and other cream sweets.

Rubber fondant mats These are sheets of rubber with shaped impressions into which fondants, jellies and chocolates are poured and allowed to set.

11

They can be obtained from most good hardware stores, but if you have difficulty, we give addresses of stockists on page 125.

Caramel bars These are used for toffee and caramel making. They are small bar shaped moulds that can be adjusted to give the exact size and thickness required. Unless you inherited them from your grandmother, or have found some in a junk shop, you may well have difficulty in obtaining them nowadays: they come into the category of optional extras and you can turn out perfectly good caramels and toffees without them.

Caramel markers Different sizes of squares can be used to mark toffees and fudges before they are set. They mark the toffee into neat pieces so that it may easily be cut with a sharp knife when set.

Other Useful Items
Skewers and cocktail sticks are useful for dipping and for tricky bits of intricate decoration. Have lolly sticks to hand, and larger wooden sticks for lollipops. Airtight polythene containers or tins are essential for short term storage and cling film is very useful for covering the surface of sweets and chocolates. Waxed and greaseproof paper and small sweet cases are necessary for presentation and protection. Details on how to pack and wrap are given on pages 111–125.

INGREDIENTS

One of the advantages of making your own sweets is that you know all the ingredients are pure and fresh and that there are no artificial additives. Most of the ingredients are found in the kitchen or are easily obtainable.

Sugar This is a most important ingredient in sweet making. Each of the different sugars has its own characteristics, and the way in which it is used affects the texture of the finished sweets.

Granulated sugar is suitable for many recipes as it dissolves easily, but it gives a slightly coarse texture to uncooked fondants and marzipan. Preserving or lump sugar is used when a clear syrup without scum is required. It has the added advantage of being less likely to burn. Caster sugar gives a finer texture and is suitable for recipes where it is necessary to dissolve the sugar quickly. Icing sugar is the finest of the white sugars and should be used when a very fine texture is required, for example for smooth fondants, fudges and marzipans.

Rich brown soft sugar gives toffees a good dark colour and a rich flavour. Light brown soft sugar is used for fudges when a finer texture and mild syrupy flavour are required. Demerara sugar also gives toffees and fudges a good syrupy flavour, but it should only be used in recipes where a high enough cooking temperature ensures that this coarser type of sugar is thoroughly dissolved.

Butter Unsalted butter gives the best results. Small amounts of margarine can be substituted, but a lot is not easily absorbed into mixtures.

Glucose Glucose is often added to fondant mixtures as it helps to prevent crystallisation. It can be purchased in powdered or liquid form from large chemists and both kinds keep almost indefinitely. Manufacturers' instructions should be followed, though the recipes themselves give exact quantities.

Milk Evaporated or condensed milk give good results and flavour in many recipes.

Flavourings Natural flavourings are available in the form of extracts and essences. Extracts are available from good chemist shops and wholesalers and are more concentrated and have a stronger and better flavour than essences. Add very few drops at a time and taste the mixture for flavour as you go.

Useful flavours for sweet making are almond, vanilla, strawberry, raspberry, ratafia, peppermint, orange and lemon. Fruit juices give a good flavour but are generally not concentrated enough and can make mixtures too moist.

Brandy, rum and Maraschino give richness and flavour to mixtures.

Colourings Pure vegetable food colourings are obtainable from good grocers and from specialist suppliers (see page 125), and it is easy to mix the basic colours for greater variety.

SUGAR BOILING TEMPERATURES

The boiling of the sugar – making sure the correct temperature is reached – is the secret of successful sweet making. A thermometer ensures accuracy, but simple, more homely tests can achieve good results.

Before you start Prepare the thermometer by placing it in cold water, bringing the water to the boil and leaving it in the water until required.

Dissolve the sugar in the water very slowly. Do not allow it to boil until completely dissolved.

Once the sugar is boiling Remove any crystals that form on the sides of the pan with a clean brush dipped in hot water.
Resist the temptation to stir the syrup unless the recipe actually tells you to do so.

Test for the correct temperature by placing the thermometer in the saucepan so that the syrup covers the bulb. If the thermometer has a sliding clip, it should be hooked over the side of the pan.

The following table gives the exact temperatures required for various types of sweet. They are usually identified by the names of the homely tests you can do to judge temperature without a thermometer.

Smooth 102–104°C (215–220°F)
This is used for crystallisation.
The mixture should begin to look syrupy. Dip the fingers into cold water and then quickly into the syrup. The thumb will slide smoothly over the fingers but still feel sugary.

Soft ball 113–118°C (235–245°F)
This is used for fondants and fudges.
To test without a thermometer, place a small drop of the syrup into cold water. If rolled with the fingers the syrup should form a soft ball.

Hard ball 118–130°C (245–265°F)
This is used for caramels, nougats and marshmallows.
To test without a thermometer, drop a small amount of the syrup into cold water and the small ball which forms should be hard enough to hold its shape.

Soft crack 132–143°C (270–290°F)
This is used for toffee.
When dropped into cold water, it separates into threads which become hard but not brittle.

Hard crack 149–154°C (300–310°F)
This is used for hard toffee and rock.
A drop in cold water separates into threads which become hard and brittle.

Caramel 154°C (310°F)
This is used for making praline and caramels.
Colouring is the best indication. It changes from a light golden to a darker brown colour.

Fancy a Fondant?

Uncooked and boiled fondants

These soft creamy sweets can be given pretty colourings and an unlimited variety of fancy shapes. They are delicious in their own right, but also make excellent centres for chocolates. There are two kinds of fondants – uncooked and boiled.

Uncooked fondant is very simply made and is ideal for beginners or children. Endless variations can be made from one basic mixture by dividing it and adding different flavourings and food colourings. Roll out the fondant on a surface dusted with sifted icing sugar and use small cutters or a knife to shape. Uncooked fondants become dry and brittle very quickly; the addition of glucose or cream of tartar helps to keep them soft and extend their storage life.

Boiled fondant is for more advanced sweetmakers. You need a lot of practice to judge the correct temperature before 'turning' the fondant and kneading the mixture for a perfect smooth finish. The addition of cream of tartar or glucose helps to prevent crystallisation. (Fondants made with glucose remain soft longer than those made with cream of tartar.)

When making boiled fondant for immediate use it should be poured on to a marble, enamel or wooden surface that has been dampened with cold water, or else poured into a wet bowl, and

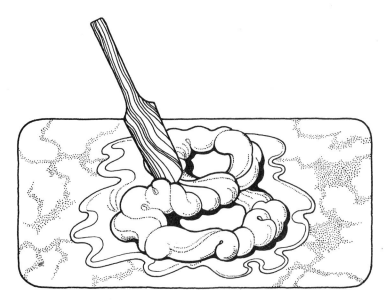

Turning boiled fondant, using a figure of eight movement, to achieve a smooth texture

Fondant fancies (*page 22*), Almond creams (*page 23*), Orange dreams (*page 19*), Coffee walnut lumps (*page 18*) ▶

allowed to stand for 10–15 minutes. A skin will form round the edge and this is the moment to start 'turning' the fondant. If the temperature is too hot the texture of the fondant will be gritty. It takes longer to 'turn' a cooler mixture but the result will be a smoother, finer fondant.

Food colourings and flavourings should be added very carefully and kneaded in evenly.

Boiled fondant may be rolled out thinly and cut out in the same way as uncooked fondant. For a really professional finish the fondant can be melted down again after turning, poured into starch trays or rubber moulds and left to set (see the directions for Fondant fancies on page 22). Once set these fondants may be 'dipped' in melted chocolate (see page 103) or decorated with crystallised flower petals, nuts, glacé fruits, etc.

To store fondants, put them in small sweet cases and pack them in airtight containers.

Uncooked fondant

This basic fondant can be rolled out and cut into fancy shapes using a small cutter to make simple sweets.

450 g (1 lb) icing sugar, sifted
45 ml (3 tbsp) liquid glucose or good pinch cream of tartar
1 egg white, lightly whisked
few drops of flavouring
few drops of food colouring

Place the icing sugar and glucose or cream of tartar in a bowl and add sufficient egg white to make a pliable mixture. Knead it thoroughly on a surface dusted with icing sugar and add a few drops of flavouring and colouring. Roll out and use as required.
Makes about 450 g (1 lb)

Cream fondant

This slightly richer version of plain fondant can be used in a similar way.

450 g (1 lb) icing sugar
2.5 ml (½ level tsp) cream of tartar
30 ml (2 tbsp) single cream
1 egg white, lightly whisked

Sift together the icing sugar and cream of tartar and add the cream and sufficient egg white to mix to a pliable paste. Knead for 5 minutes on a surface lightly dusted with icing sugar, then cover and leave for 1 hour before using.
Makes about 450 g (1 lb)

◀ Cherry bon-bons (*page 25*), Fondant fruits (*page 26*)

Lemon creams

few drops of yellow food colouring
few drops of lemon essence
225 g (8 oz) cream fondant (see page 17)
crystallised lemon peel to decorate

Knead the colouring and essence into the freshly made fondant, cover and leave for 1 hour to mellow. Roll out on a surface lightly dusted with icing sugar, cut into semi-circles and put a small piece of crystallised lemon peel on each for decoration. Leave the lemon creams for 24 hours until thoroughly dry.
Makes about 225 g (8 oz)

Coffee walnut lumps

Illustrated in colour facing page 16

450 g (1 lb) icing sugar, sifted
30 ml (2 tbsp) condensed milk
15 ml (1 tbsp) coffee essence or strong black coffee
about 30 ml (2 tbsp) water
walnut halves to decorate

In a bowl, mix the icing sugar with the condensed milk, coffee essence and water to a very stiff but pliable consistency. Divide into small, even-sized pieces, sprinkle the hands with a little icing sugar and shape the fondant into balls. Flatten slightly, press half a walnut on each ball and leave in a warm, dry place until firm.
Makes about 450 g (1 lb)

Date cream bars

450 g (1 lb) icing sugar, sifted
juice of $\frac{1}{2}$ lemon
100 g (4 oz) stoned dates, chopped
$\frac{1}{2}$ egg white, lightly whisked
few drops of red food colouring
about 5 ml (1 tsp) water to mix

In a bowl, mix the icing sugar with the lemon juice and dates. Add the egg white, colouring and water and mix to a very stiff paste. Leave to stand for 1 hour, then roll out to 1 cm ($\frac{1}{2}$ in) thick on a surface lightly dusted with icing sugar. Dredge with icing sugar and cut the mixture into small, neat bars using a sharp knife.
Makes about 550 g (1$\frac{1}{4}$ lb)

Orange dreams

Illustrated in colour facing page 16

grated rind of 1 orange
30 ml (2 tbsp) orange juice
10 ml (2 tsp) lemon juice
350 g (12 oz) icing sugar, sifted
1 egg white, lightly whisked
few drops of orange food colouring
little angelica

Mix the grated orange rind and fruit juices together and add the icing sugar with sufficient egg white to give a firm but pliable consistency. Add the orange food colouring and knead well.

Shape into small balls, rub them over a fine grater to give the effect of orange skin and put a small piece of angelica on each for a stalk. Leave for 24 hours to set and dry.
Makes about 350 g (12 oz)

Peppermint creams (uncooked)

Oil of peppermint is much stronger than the essence, so if you are using it, use it sparingly!

450 g (1 lb) icing sugar, sifted
5 ml (1 tsp) lemon juice
1 egg white, lightly whisked
few drops of peppermint essence or oil of peppermint
green food colouring (optional)

In a bowl, mix the sugar with the lemon juice and enough egg white to make a pliable mixture. Flavour with peppermint and tint a very pale green if liked. Knead on a surface dusted with

icing sugar and roll out to 0.5 cm ($\frac{1}{4}$ in) thick. Cut into rounds with a 2.5-cm (1-in) cutter, or form into balls and flatten slightly with a rolling pin. Leave for 24 hours to set and dry.
Makes about 450 g (1 lb)

Rosehip creams

These delicate creams are delicious with after-dinner coffee and are best eaten within 2 days of making.

25 ml (5 tsp) lemon juice
2.5 ml ($\frac{1}{2}$ level tsp) finely grated lemon rind
20 ml (4 tsp) rosehip syrup
few drops of vanilla essence
225 g (8 oz) icing sugar, sifted
15 g ($\frac{1}{2}$ oz) crystallised rose petals to decorate

Put the lemon juice, rind, rosehip syrup and vanilla essence into a bowl. Add the icing sugar and stir until smooth, using the finger tips if necessary to achieve the consistency of a paste.

Divide into about 18 pieces, roll into balls and transfer to a surface dusted with icing sugar. Press a piece of crystallised rose petal into the centre of each ball. Refrigerate until firm, or leave to dry in a cool place.
Makes about 225 g (8 oz)

Walnut creams (uncooked)

1 egg white, lightly whisked
30 ml (2 tbsp) cold water
few drops of vanilla essence
450 g (1 lb) icing sugar, sifted
walnut halves to decorate

Put the egg white into a bowl with the water and vanilla essence, mix well and work in the sifted icing sugar to give a stiff but pliable paste. Knead until smooth then divide into small, even-sized pieces. Roll each into a ball and press a halved walnut into the top. Leave for 24 hours to set and dry.
Makes about 450 g (1 lb)

Boiled fondant

150 ml ($\frac{1}{4}$ pint) water (good measure)
450 g (1 lb) granulated sugar
45 ml (3 level tbsp) powdered glucose or good pinch cream of tartar

Heat the water and sugar gently in a heavy-based saucepan until the sugar is dissolved. Bring the syrup to the boil, add the glucose or cream of tartar and boil to 116°C (240°F) (soft ball stage). Sprinkle a little water on a marble or enamel slab or wooden chopping board, pour on the syrup and leave for a few minutes to cool.

When a skin forms round the edges, use a spatula to collect the mixture together, then turn it, working it backwards and forwards using a figure-of-eight movement. Continue to work the syrup, collecting it into as small a compass as possible, until it changes its consistency and 'grains', becoming opaque and firm. Scrape it off the slab and knead it in the hands until it is even-textured throughout.

Note If no slab is available the fondant can be turned in a bowl; leave it in the bowl for 15 minutes to cool, turn it in the bowl until thick, then knead it on greaseproof paper.

Makes about 550 g (1¼ lb)

Cream fondant

The flavour and texture of boiled fondant may be improved by adding a little cream, evaporated milk or melted butter, in the proportions of 45 ml (3 tbsp) cream or milk or 50 g (2 oz) melted butter per 450 g (1 lb) of fondant. These enriching ingredients may either be kneaded into prepared fondant or added to freshly made fondant while it is still in its melted state. Additional flavourings – for example lemon, coffee, rosewater, violet, vanilla – may also be added to this fondant.

Fondant creams

Divide some cream fondant (*see above*) into equal portions and flavour and colour as liked, for example with lemon, violet and coffee. Roll out the fondant on a surface lightly dusted with icing sugar and cut out with a small cutter or model it by hand to make fancy shapes. Put the sweets into paper cases and leave to dry.

Peppermint creams (boiled)

Knead a few drops of peppermint essence or oil of peppermint into some boiled or cream fondant (*see above*) – remembering that oil of peppermint is particularly strong. Roll it out to 0.5 cm (¼ in) thick on a surface lightly dusted with icing sugar and cut into rounds with a 2.5-cm (1-in) cutter. Put into paper cases and leave to dry.

Walnut creams (boiled)

Knead a few drops of coffee essence or strong black coffee into some boiled or cream fondant (*see above*). Shape into balls about 2.5 cm (1 in) in diameter, press a half walnut into each and put the sweets into paper cases and leave to dry.

Hazel creams Knead a few drops of vanilla essence and green food colouring into some boiled or cream fondant (*see page 21*). Shape into small ovals, press a hazelnut into the centre of each and put the sweets into paper cases and leave to dry.

Fondant fancies *Illustrated in colour facing page 16*

Boiled fondant can be melted down and reset in moulds to make more interesting shapes. These 'fancies' may be decorated with nuts, glacé fruit, crystallised flowers, etc, and make attractive sweets in their own right, but they also make excellent chocolate centres. We give instructions for dipping chocolates in the chocolates chapter, on page 103.

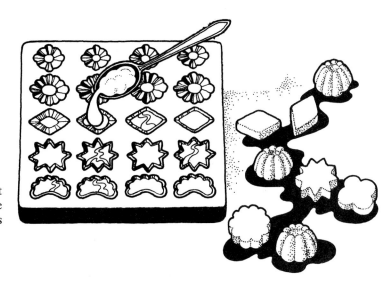

Pouring melted fondant into a fondant mat to make Fondant fancies

Melt prepared boiled fondant in a basin over a pan of hot water or in a double saucepan over a very gentle heat: use a little sugar syrup (or a few drops of water) to help to liquefy it and be careful not to overheat it as this makes the fondant rough and spoils the gloss. When it is liquid, pour it into moulds in a rubber fondant mat, or starch moulds, using a funnel or a teaspoon.

Rainbow creams 225 g (8 oz) violet flavoured cream fondant (*see page 21*)
1 egg white, lightly whisked
225 g (8 oz) unboiled marzipan (*see page 28*)
225 g (8 oz) rose flavoured cream fondant (*see page 21*)

Fancy a Fondant?

Roll out a layer of violet cream fondant to 0.5 cm ($\frac{1}{4}$ in) thick, moisten with egg white and place a layer of plain marzipan on top. Moisten again with egg white and cover with a layer of rose cream fondant. Each layer should be very flat and of a similar thickness. Roll slightly and cut into small squares, rounds or diamonds. Leave to dry for 24 hours.
Makes about 700 g ($1\frac{1}{2}$ lb)

Almond creams

Illustrated in colour facing page 16

125–175 g (4–6 oz) ground almonds
few drops of almond essence
225 g (8 oz) boiled fondant (*see page 20*)
few drops of green food colouring
blanched or unblanched almonds to decorate

Work the ground almonds and a few drops of almond essence into the fondant, add a very little green colouring and let it stand for 1 hour. Roll out on a surface lightly dusted with icing sugar, cut into bars and decorate each with a whole almond. Leave to dry for 24 hours.
Makes about 350 g (12 oz)

Chocolate fondants

100 g (4 oz) plain chocolate, finely grated
225 g (8 oz) boiled fondant (*see page 20*)
few drops of vanilla essence
crystallised violets, pistachio nuts, etc to decorate

Melt the chocolate in a bowl over a pan of hot water and allow to cool slightly. Hollow out the fondant, put the chocolate and essence into the centre and knead thoroughly, using a dusting of icing sugar to prevent the fondant sticking and to make it easier to handle. Leave for 1 hour.

Roll out the fondant and cut into neat squares. Decorate with a small piece of crystallised violet or rose leaf, or a pistachio nut. Allow to dry for 24 hours.
Makes about 350 g (12 oz)

Coconut creams

few drops of vanilla essence
100 g (4 oz) desiccated coconut
225 g (8 oz) boiled fondant (*see page 20*)
few drops of red food colouring
caster sugar

Knead the vanilla and coconut into the fondant. Divide in half and colour one half a pale pink by working in a little of the red food colouring. Roll each piece into a strip 0.5 cm (¼ in) thick and place the pink one on top of the white. Press together with the rolling pin, sprinkle with caster sugar and allow to dry for 24 hours. Cut into small bars.

Makes about 350 g (12 oz)

Lemon nut creams

100 g (4 oz) shelled hazelnuts or almonds, chopped
few drops of lemon essence
225 g (8 oz) boiled fondant (*see page 20*)

Knead the nuts and a few drops of essence into the fondant. Roll out to about 0.5 cm (¼ in) thick and leave to dry for 24 hours. Cut into small rectangles.

Makes about 350 g (12 oz)

Tangerine creams

5 ml (1 tsp) grated tangerine rind
few drops of orange food colouring
225 g (8 oz) boiled fondant (*see page 20*)
few cloves
lemonade crystals or powdered lemon sherbet

Work the tangerine rind and a little food colouring into the fondant. Knead well and allow to stand 1 hour before using.

Shape into balls and roll these over a fine grater to give the effect of tangerine skin. Stick a clove into each to represent the calyx. Roll the ball in lemonade crystals and allow to dry for 24 hours.

Makes about 225 g (8 oz)

Violet creams

few drops of violet essence
few drops of violet food colouring
225 g (8 oz) boiled fondant (*see page 20*)
crystallised violets to decorate

Knead the violet essence and food colouring into the fondant and allow to stand for 1 hour before using. Shape into balls, flatten slightly with a rolling pin and place a small piece of crystallised violet on the centre of each. Allow to dry for 24 hours.

Makes about 225 g (8 oz)

24

Chocolate fondant whirls

225 g (8 oz) boiled fondant (*see page 20*)
25 g (1 oz) plain or milk chocolate

Knead the boiled fondant until smooth and soft, then divide it into two portions. Melt the chocolate in a bowl over a pan of hot water and mix it with half the fondant, then roll this out into a rectangle and trim the edges. Roll out the white fondant into a rectangle of the same length and width and place it on top of the chocolate one.

Roll up from the long edge, like a Swiss roll, pressing it into a sausage shape. Cut into slices 0.5 cm ($\frac{1}{4}$ in) thick.
Makes about 225 g (8 oz)

Cherry bon-bons

Illustrated in colour facing page 17

boiled fondant (*see page 20*)
few drops of pink food colouring optional
few drops of Maraschino flavouring
little water
whole glacé cherries

Put the fondant into a basin and melt it over boiling water. Colour and flavour it and thin it down slightly with a few drops of water, until it will coat a wooden spoon easily but not too thickly. Remove the pan from the heat, then, working quickly, use a skewer to dip the cherries into the liquid fondant. Put them on greaseproof paper to set and serve the cherries in paper cases.

Note Overheating the fondant makes it lose its shine, while removing it from the heat means that it quickly starts to set; so it is wisest to use only small quantities of fondant at a time – and even then it is essential to work quickly. For variety, flavour one batch of fondant with coffee and use to dip almonds, halved walnuts, whole Brazils or other dessert nuts.

Opera creams

Maraschino gives these fondants a delicate colour and sophisticated flavour: use other liqueurs and appropriate food colourings to make a selection.

450 g (1 lb) preserving sugar
150 ml (¼ pint) water
90 ml (6 level tbsp) powdered glucose
few drops of Maraschino
15 ml (1 tbsp) single cream
little icing sugar, sifted

Heat the sugar, water and glucose gently in a heavy-based saucepan, stirring all the time until the sugar is dissolved. Skim when necessary and brush any scum or crystals from the sides of the pan with a brush dipped in cold water. Boil without stirring to 116°C (240°F) (soft ball stage), then pour on to a wetted slab or large dish.

Turn until it is opaque, using first a wooden spoon or spatula, then the hands. Hollow out slightly and work in the Maraschino and cream, together with sufficient icing sugar to make the right consistency for shaping. Roll out to 2.5-cm (1-in) thick square, using a little icing sugar to prevent it sticking. Leave it until cold, then cut into squares with a sharp knife or caramel cutter.
Makes about 450 g (1 lb)

Coconut kisses

450 g (1 lb) granulated sugar
100 g (4 oz) powdered glucose
150 ml (¼ pint) water
175 g (6 oz) desiccated coconut
few drops of food colouring (optional)

Put the sugar, glucose and water into a pan and heat gently until the sugar has dissolved, then boil to 116°C (240°F) (soft ball stage). Remove from the heat and stir in the coconut. If liked, use a few drops of food colouring to tint the mixture, then form it into small rocky heaps on waxed paper and leave to cool.
Makes about 700 g (1½ lb)

Fondant fruits

Illustrated in colour facing page 17

Use the same liquid fondant as for Cherry bon-bons (*see page 25*) to dip fresh, crystallised or dried fruits, placing them on greaseproof paper to set. Try cubes of crystallised ginger, glacé pineapple, bunches of raisins or grapes or Cape gooseberries and serve the fruits in paper cases.

Mouthwatering Marzipan

Using bought and homemade marzipan to cut and mould

Marzipan is endlessly versatile. It absorbs flavours and colours with ease and can be moulded or cut into a huge variety of rich, pretty and festive sweets. The natural flavour of the ground almonds in the marzipan can be enhanced by the addition of a little almond essence. Alternatively, orange flower water or rose water, available in single, double or triple strength from most good chemists, will give the marzipan a delicately refreshing flavour if added in small quantities. As with fondant, it may either be uncooked or cooked.

Uncooked marzipan is simple enough for a child to make, and with imaginative use of colourings and flavourings can be cut into interesting sweets. What it's not much good for is any complicated moulding as it cracks badly with too much kneading and handling.

Cooked marzipan is easier to mould than uncooked, and bought marzipan can also be used once it has been softened by kneading for a few minutes. Use cooked marzipan for moulding round fruits and nuts and for making into flowers and fruits. As long as an adult supervises the cooking of the marzipan, children can have hours of fun using it to make marzipan animals. Once made, cooked marzipan can be stored for weeks wrapped in greaseproof paper and sealed in a polythene bag. If it does dry out a bit, it can be softened by kneading in a little egg white.

To store marzipan sweets, place them in small sweet cases and pack in airtight tins. It is important to pack them loosely and to keep them separate from each other so that the colours don't rub off. Marzipan sweets will keep well for several weeks.

Simple marzipan or almond paste (unboiled)

Using this unboiled marzipan, or bought almond paste, you can produce a surprisingly wide variety of attractive sweets. The marzipan may be tinted with edible colourings, combined with nuts, dried or glacé fruits, etc, flavoured in various ways and cut or moulded into different shapes.

225 g (8 oz) icing sugar, sifted
225 g (8 oz) caster sugar
450 g (1 lb) ground almonds
5 ml (1 tsp) vanilla essence
2 standard eggs, lightly beaten
lemon juice

Mix the icing sugar with the caster sugar and ground almonds. Add the essence, with sufficient egg and lemon juice to mix to a stiff dough. Form into a ball and knead lightly.
Makes 900 g (2 lb)

Boiled marzipan

450 g (1 lb) preserving sugar
150 ml ($\frac{1}{4}$ pint) water
pinch cream of tartar
350 g (12 oz) ground almonds
2 egg whites
75 g (3 oz) icing sugar, sifted

In a heavy-based saucepan, dissolve the sugar in the water over a low heat. When the syrup reaches boiling point, add the cream of tartar and boil to a temperature of 116°C (240°F) (soft ball stage). Remove the pan from the heat and stir rapidly until the syrup begins to 'grain'. Stir in the ground almonds and egg whites and cook for a few minutes over a low heat, stirring well.

Pour on to an oiled marble or enamel slab or wooden chopping board, add the icing sugar and work well with a palette knife, lifting the edges of the mixture and turning them into the centre. As soon as the mixture is sufficiently cool, knead it until smooth. Additional icing sugar may be kneaded in if the mixture is too wet.

Note This marzipan may be wrapped in greaseproof paper and stored in a cool place for 2–3 weeks.

Chocolate marzipan

75 g (3 oz) caster sugar
75 g (3 oz) icing sugar, sifted
175 g (6 oz) ground almonds
50 g (2 oz) plain chocolate, grated
15 ml (1 tbsp) hot water
$\frac{1}{2}$ beaten egg
5 ml (1 tsp) lemon juice
2.5 ml ($\frac{1}{2}$ tsp) vanilla essence

Mix the sugars thoroughly then stir in the ground almonds. Melt the chocolate in the water, in a bowl over hot water and add to the ground almond mixture. Combine the egg, lemon juice and vanilla essence, then add to the chocolate mixture. Knead well, adding extra lemon juice if required. This chocolate coloured marzipan is ideal for shaping into 'brownish' vegetables or fruits, or it can simply be cut into bars. Roll the sweets in caster sugar and allow to dry.
Makes about 350 g (12 oz)

Marzipan mushrooms

15 ml (1 level tbsp) cocoa powder
10 ml (2 tsp) hot water
225 g (8 oz) marzipan

Dissolve the cocoa in the water, then knead this into half the marzipan. Break off pieces of the uncoloured paste and form into mushroom caps. Press a flat piece of the coloured paste into each cap and use a fork to mark the gills. Make stalks from the remaining coloured paste.
Makes about 18

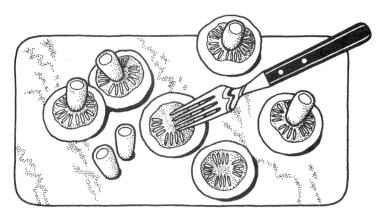

Use a fork to mark the gills of marzipan mushrooms

Nutty cherry whirls

Illustrated in colour facing page 32

450 g (1 lb) marzipan
few drops of green food colouring
few drops of pistachio flavouring
15 g ($\frac{1}{2}$ oz) cocoa powder
100 g (4 oz) glacé cherries
100 g (4 oz) chocolate, melted
100 g (4 oz) blanched almonds, chopped and toasted

Divide the marzipan into three. Add green food colouring and pistachio flavouring to one piece and blend the cocoa into another. Roll out each piece to a strip about 0.3 cm ($\frac{1}{8}$ in) thick and 6.5 cm ($2\frac{1}{2}$ in) wide. Place one on top of the other, the white strip at the bottom and the chocolate-coloured strip on top.

Place a line of glacé cherries along the length and roll up from the long edge as if making a Swiss roll. Brush with the melted chocolate, then roll in the toasted almonds. Put in a cool place to harden, then cut into 1-cm ($\frac{1}{2}$-in) slices.

Note These sweets can be made up to 1 week in advance if the whole roll is wrapped in waxed paper, foil or cling film and left unsliced until required.
Makes about 800 g (1$\frac{3}{4}$ lb)

Marzipan logs

Make a thin roll of pink marzipan and roll out a strip of green marzipan the same length as the roll and wide enough to go right round it. Brush lightly with egg white and cover the pink roll with the green paste. Cut into small logs, coat with melted chocolate and roll in desiccated coconut which has been coloured pale green with green food colouring.

Marzipan walnuts

Illustrated in colour facing page 32

225 g (8 oz) marzipan
15 ml (1 level tbsp) chopped walnuts
few drops of food colouring
few halved walnuts

Knead the marzipan and work in the chopped nuts and food colouring. Shape into balls, flatten slightly and decorate each with a walnut half.
Makes about 225 g (8 oz)

Cherry balls

Roll marzipan into balls and press a glacé cherry firmly into each.

Marzipan cherries

Illustrated in colour on the jacket

Take some large glacé cherries and surround each with a strip of marzipan, so that the cherry shows top and bottom.

Harlequin marzipans

Illustrated in colour opposite

You may want to make a fresh batch of marzipan especially for these attractive sweets, but they are a particularly good way of using up small amounts left over from other recipes. Colour several equal portions of marzipan with different food colours, for example pink, green and chocolate. Roll out into strips about 0.5 cm ($\frac{1}{4}$ in) thick, brush lightly with egg white and place on top of one another. Press well together, trim the edges, then cut into squares. Roll in caster sugar and leave to dry. (The trimmings can be rolled to make harlequin balls.)

Neapolitan slices

Illustrated in colour opposite

Divide some marzipan into three equal pieces and knead a few drops of contrasting food colourings into two of them. Roll out the coloured marzipan into strips 1 cm ($\frac{1}{2}$ in) deep and about 2.5 cm (1 in) wide. Cut each strip in half lengthways and trim with a sharp knife so that they are exactly the same size.

Roll out the uncoloured piece of marzipan very thinly so that it is the same length as the strips and about 11.5 cm ($4\frac{1}{2}$ in) wide. Lay the coloured bars along it, two underneath and two on top to make a chequered pattern, and wrap the uncoloured marzipan round the bars so that the whole thing resembles a small Battenberg cake. Cut into 0.5-cm ($\frac{1}{4}$-in) slices.

Wrap the uncoloured piece of marzipan around the coloured bars before cutting Neapolitan slices

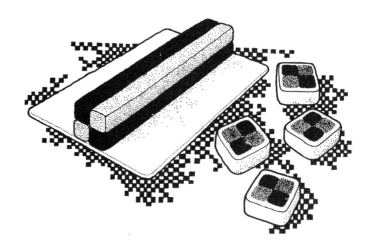

Nutty cherry whirls, Marzipan walnuts (*page 31*), Harlequin marzipans, Neapolitan slices (above), Marzipan triangles, Stuffed dates (*page 33*) ▶

Marzipan triangles

Illustrated in colour facing page 32

Tint two equal portions of marzipan with contrasting food colour-ings. Form one into a 2.5-cm (1-in) triangular bar; roll the other into a rectangle the same length as the bar and 9 cm (3½ in) wide. Position the bar along the rectangle and wrap the flat piece of marzipan right round the bar so that there is a contrasting strip round the outside. You should now have a bar of the same triangular shape but it will of course be larger. Cut the bar into 1-cm (½-in) slices.

Stuffed dates and plums

Illustrated in colour facing page 32

Choose good quality dessert dates. Remove the stones and fill the cavities with coloured marzipan. Roll the dates in caster sugar and put them into paper cases.

Small plums may be used in the same way, or good-sized prunes, thoroughly soaked.

Marzipan fruits and flowers

To make fruits, take small balls of boiled marzipan and mould them into the desired shapes with the fingers. Using a small paint brush and food colourings, tint them all over or add shading, as necessary. (If making one variety of fruit only, it is easier to add the food colouring to the marzipan before shaping.) Finish off as follows:

Oranges and other citrus fruit: To obtain a pitted surface, roll the fruit lightly on the finest part of a grater.

Strawberries and raspberries: roll them in sifted caster or icing sugar to give them a bumpy surface.

◀ Turkish delight (*page 37*)

Apples and pears: use a clove, or part only of its stalk, or a piece of angelica to represent the stalk.

Marzipan vegetables can be made in a similar way, though it may be easier and more realistic when making brown 'earthy' vegetables, like potatoes, to dust them with a little chocolate powder instead of painting them.

Flowers: roll out the almond paste thinly and cut it into rounds, using a 2–2.5-cm ($\frac{3}{4}$–1-in) cutter. Mould these rounds into leaves or petals and fix them together with a little egg white to form flowers. Leaves may also be made from angelica. Leave until quite dry, then paint them with a little food colouring, applied with a small brush.

Note Boiled marzipan is also ideal for modelling animals and we give directions in the 'Novelties' chapter, on pages 52 and 53.

Jolly Jellies –
and Jellied Sweets

*Gelatine-based sweets, candied,
crystallised and glacé fruits*

In this chapter we have put together a mixture of traditional fruit jellies and gelatine-based sweets such as Turkish delight and Crèmes de menthe. We also give instructions for how to make exotic (and expensive to buy) candied, crystallised and glacé fruits.

Fruit jellies are very easy to make and can be varied by adding different flavours and colours to the basic jelly. For professional looking results, the liquid jelly mixture can be poured into dampened rubber fondant mats and left to set. Remove the jellies by loosening the edges of each jelly and carefully peeling back the flexible rubber mat. The jellies can be left plain or tossed in granulated sugar.

All jelly based sweets use gelatine and this needs careful handling. Powdered gelatine should be dissolved by first mixing with a little cold water in a small bowl then standing the bowl in a pan of hot water until the mixture becomes clear and syrupy.

In some gelatine based sweets, gelatine is used to replace egg white and will bind the ingredients together as well as acting as a setting agent. Jelly type sweets should be cut and tossed in icing sugar, then stored in an airtight box lined with waxed paper. If stored in a dry place they should keep for several weeks.

Candying fruits is a method of preserving using a sugar syrup. The fruit is soaked in the syrup, of which the sugar content is increased each day until the fruits are completely saturated. A crystallised or a glacé finish requires one more easy stage. These festive and delicious sweetmeats keep indefinitely in airtight glass jars.

Fresh fruit jellies

Illustrated in colour on the jacket

150 ml ($\frac{1}{4}$ pint) fruit juice (lemon, orange, blackcurrant, etc)
about 75 g (3 oz) granulated sugar
90 ml (6 level tbsp) powdered glucose
25 g (1 oz) powdered gelatine
caster sugar

Have ready a 15-cm (6-in) square tin. Put the fruit juice in a saucepan with sufficient sugar to sweeten and dissolve the sugar over a low heat. Add the glucose and gelatine and heat gently

Before cutting up jellied sweets, turn out the mixture by dipping the tin quickly into hot water

until the gelatine has dissolved. Dampen the tin, pour in the fruit juice mixture and leave to set. Turn the jelly out by dipping the tin in hot water for a few seconds, then cut it into cubes or fancy shapes. Roll the sweets in caster sugar.
Makes about 225 g (8 oz)

Notes If the mixture is very pale, the sweets can be made more attractive by adding a few drops of food colouring.
The jellies may be made in small moulds, rubber mats or starch moulds, if available.

Turkish delight

Illustrated in colour facing page 33

This recipe produces a Turkish delight very similar to the genuine Oriental variety, but it is impossible to get identical results without the authentic ingredients.

450 g (1 lb) granulated sugar
900 ml (1½ pints) water
1.25 ml (¼ level tsp) cream of tartar
75 g (3 oz) cornflour
200 g (7 oz) icing sugar
50 g (2 oz) honey
few drops of lemon essence
few drops of rosewater
few drops of pink food colouring
icing sugar for dredging

Butter an 18-cm (7-in) square tin. Put the sugar and 150 ml (¼ pint) of the water into a saucepan, stir to dissolve the sugar, then bring to a temperature of 113–118°C (235–245°F) (soft ball

37

stage). Add the cream of tartar and remove from the heat.

Mix the cornflour and icing sugar with a little of the remaining cold water. Boil the rest of the water, then pour on to the blended cornflour and sugar, stirring hard to prevent lumps forming. Return to the saucepan and simmer, beating vigorously, until clear and thick.

Add the syrup gradually, beating over the heat. Continue to boil for 30 minutes: it is essential that the character of the starch be changed by the prolonged boiling with the acid. After 30 minutes the mixture should be a pale transparent straw colour.

Add the honey and flavourings and blend thoroughly, then pour half the mixture into the buttered tin. Colour the remainder a pale rose pink and pour it on top of the mixture already in the tin. Leave until quite cold. Dip a sharp knife into icing sugar and cut the mixture into neat pieces. Toss in icing sugar, then cover and leave in the sugar for at least 24 hours. Pack in boxes in a generous quantity of icing sugar.

Makes about 700 g (1½ lb)

Variation
Pour the plain and coloured syrups into separate tins to set.

Quick Turkish delight

300 ml (½ pint) hot water
25 g (1 oz) powdered gelatine
450 g (1 lb) granulated sugar
1.25 ml (¼ level tsp) citric acid
few drops of vanilla essence
few drops of almond essence
red food colouring
50 g (2 oz) icing sugar
25 g (1 oz) cornflour

Have ready a 20.5 × 15-cm (8 × 6-in) tin. Put the water in a heavy-based saucepan. Sprinkle the gelatine over it, add the sugar and citric acid and heat slowly until the sugar has dissolved. Bring to the boil and boil for 20 minutes.

Remove from the heat and leave to stand for 10 minutes without stirring. Add the flavourings and pour half the mixture into the tin. Add a few drops of food colouring to the second half and pour over the first layer. Leave in a cool place for 24 hours.

Sift the icing sugar and cornflour together and sprinkle it evenly over a piece of greaseproof paper. Turn the Turkish delight out on to this paper and cut it into squares with a sharp knife. Toss well in the sugar mixture, then pack in greaseproof paper and store in an airtight tin.

Makes about 550 g (1¼ lb)

Abricotines

300 ml (½ pint) apricot purée
225 g (8 oz) granulated sugar
10–15 ml (2–3 tsp) lemon juice
granulated or caster sugar to coat

Have ready a 20.5 × 15-cm (8 × 6-in) tin. Make the purée from about 450 g (1 lb) canned or fresh fruit, or from 225 g (8 oz) dried fruit, soaked and cooked. Put the purée, sugar and lemon juice into a heavy-based saucepan and dissolve the sugar over a gentle heat, then bring the mixture to the boil and cook, stirring gently, for about 40 minutes, or until a little will set firmly on a cold surface.

Wet the tin and pour in the mixture. When the jelly is set, cut it into pieces and roll them in caster or granulated sugar. Store in an airtight jar or other container.
Makes about 450 g (1 lb)

Notes Abricotines may also be set in peppermint cream rings on a wetted marble or enamel surface.
This recipe can also be used for jujubes made from such fruit as peaches, raspberries or blackcurrants.

Crèmes de menthe

Illustrated in colour facing page 56

The most festive and sophisticated of after-dinner mints.

25 g (1 oz) gum arabic
45–60 ml (3–4 tbsp) water
50 g (2 oz) cornflour
450 g (1 lb) granulated sugar
150 ml (¼ pint) water
25 g (1 oz) powdered gelatine
few drops of green food colouring
few drops of peppermint essence
icing sugar, sifted

Have ready a 20.5 × 15-cm (8 × 6-in) tin. Dissolve the gum arabic in the water and blend the cornflour with a little extra cold water. Put the sugar, 150 ml (¼ pint) water and gelatine into a heavy-based saucepan and bring to the boil; add the gum arabic and cornflour solutions, re-boil and cook for 10 minutes, stirring. Add a little colouring and flavouring. Dampen the tin, pour in the peppermint mixture and leave to set. Turn the jelly out by dipping the tin in hot water for a few seconds, then cut it into squares and roll these in the icing sugar.
Makes about 450 g (1 lb)

Raspberry jellies

350 g (12 oz) granulated sugar
150 ml ($\frac{1}{4}$ pint) cold water
20 g ($\frac{3}{4}$ oz) powdered gelatine
60 ml (4 tbsp) hot water
few drops of raspberry essence
few drops of red food colouring
icing sugar, sifted

Dampen a 20.5 × 10-cm (8 × 4-in) tin. In a heavy-based saucepan, dissolve the sugar in the cold water over a gentle heat and boil to 116°C (240°F) (soft ball stage). Dissolve the gelatine in the hot water.

Add the essence and food colouring to the syrup and stir in the gelatine. Pour it into the dampened tin; it should not be more than about 2.5 cm (1 in) in depth. Leave it in a cool place to set, then cut the jelly into cubes with a sharp knife and roll these in icing sugar.

Makes about 350 g (12 oz)

Variations
Other fruit essences, or flavourings such as peppermint, may also be used, together with appropriate colours, and the shapes of the sweets can be varied, for instance, by cutting the jelly into rounds using a 2-cm ($\frac{3}{4}$-in) cutter.

Fruit bars

An unusual and delicious type of sweetmeat, which is also satisfying and full of vitamins. This is a useful recipe for when you have a glut of ripe fruit.

Choose fully ripe fruit and simmer it until soft in just enough water to prevent it from burning. (Remove the peel from citrus fruit before cooking.) Sieve it to remove pips and skin, etc, and add sugar to taste (except in the case of ripe dessert pears which should be sweet enough).

Now simmer the sweetened pulp gently, stirring constantly until it is really thick. Spread it out on a baking tin and dry slowly, either in the oven, at the lowest setting, or in a warm place. This may take from a few hours to 2–3 days, depending on the method used.

When the fruit pulp is firm enough to handle, cut it into small bars, squares or rounds and roll the pieces in caster sugar. Store in a screw-top jar.

Note To vary the sweets, add suitable spices or flavourings, or a little red, green or yellow food colouring.

Ginger jellies

20 g (¾ oz) powdered gelatine
100 ml (4 fl oz) cold water
400 g (14 oz) caster sugar
50 ml (2 fl oz) hot water
15 ml (1 tbsp) lemon juice
100 g (4 oz) crystallised ginger, chopped
50 g (2 oz) cornflour
50 g (2 oz) icing sugar, sifted

Have ready a 15-cm (6-in) square tin. Soak the gelatine in the cold water. Dissolve the sugar in the hot water and boil together for 10 minutes in a heavy-based saucepan. Add the soaked gelatine and boil for another 15 minutes.

Add the lemon juice and ginger, cool, then pour into the wetted tin and leave to set for 24 hours. Cut into neat squares and allow to dry for a few hours. Dust with the mixed cornflour and icing sugar.

Makes about 450 g (1 lb)

Fig jellies

25 g (1 oz) powdered gelatine
150 ml (¼ pint) water
175 g (6 oz) granulated sugar
juice of ½ a lemon
grated rind and juice of ½ an orange
25 g (1 oz) nuts, chopped
50 g (2 oz) figs, chopped
50 g (2 oz) cornflour
50 g (2 oz) icing sugar, sifted

Have ready a 15-cm (6-in) square tin. Dissolve the gelatine in half the water. In a heavy-based saucepan bring the rest of the water, the sugar and the lemon and orange juice to the boil. Add the nuts, figs and orange rind to the syrup and boil together for 20 minutes.

Add the dissolved gelatine and re-boil for 10 minutes. Pour the mixture into the wetted tin and allow to set for 24 hours. Cut the jelly into small squares and dust with the mixed cornflour and icing sugar. Allow to dry for a few hours.

Makes about 350 g (12 oz)

Note These sweets begin to seep if kept for a long period, so eat them up within a few days of making.

Orange and lemon slices

Illustrated in colour facing page 56

150 ml (¼ pint) fresh orange or lemon juice
175 g (6 oz) caster sugar
90 ml (6 level tbsp) powdered glucose
25 g (1 oz) powdered gelatine
granulated sugar

Have ready a 20.5-cm (8-in) square tin. Put the fruit juice and sugar into a saucepan and dissolve the sugar over a low heat. Add the glucose and gelatine and heat gently until the gelatine has dissolved.

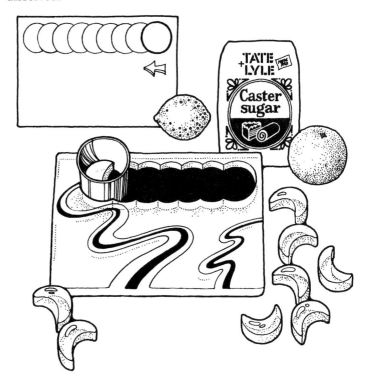

Cutting crescent shapes from the turned out fruit jelly to make Orange and lemon slices

Wet the tin and pour in the syrup. When it is firm, turn it out and cut into crescent shapes, using a 4-cm (1½-in) round cutter (see line drawing). Roll the sweets in granulated sugar if liked.
Makes about 225 g (8 oz)

Blackcurrant jujubes

300 ml (½ pint) blackcurrant purée
25 g (1 oz) powdered gelatine
100 g (4 oz) granulated sugar
150 ml (¼ pint) water
caster sugar

Have ready a 15-cm (6-in) square tin. Put all the ingredients into a heavy-based saucepan and carefully dissolve the gelatine and sugar over a gentle heat. Bring the mixture to the boil and boil for 5 minutes. Pour it into the wetted tin and leave it until firmly set. Cut the jelly into rounds, using a small round cutter, then roll the sweets in caster sugar, coating them evenly.
Makes about 225 g (8 oz)

Variations
Gooseberry and raspberry jujubes can be made by substituting the appropriate fruit purée.

Candied, crystallised and glacé fruits

Candying is a method of preserving fruits by the use of sugar syrup. They can then be served as a dessert or eaten as sweets. The peel of such citrus fruits as oranges and lemons can also be candied and is widely used in making cakes, cookies and puddings and in mincemeat and so on. We give a recipe on page 46.

Candying essentially consists of soaking the fruit in a syrup, the sugar content of which is increased daily over a stated period of time until the fruits are completely impregnated with sugar. They can then be left plain or be given a crystallised or glacé finish.

Candied fruits are expensive to buy because of the labour involved and the amount of sugar used. The process should not however be beyond the skill of the home cook, provided certain basic rules are followed.

The most suitable fruits to treat are those with a really distinctive flavour – pineapple, peaches, plums, apricots, oranges, cherries, crab-apples, pears. Both fresh and canned fruits may be used, but different types should not be candied in the same syrup.

Preparation of the fruit and syrup
Fresh fruit The fruits must be ripe, but firm and free from blemishes. Prepare them according to kind. Small whole crab-apples, apricots and plums should be pricked all over with a stainless fork; cherries must be stoned; peaches and pears are peeled and halved or cut into quarters. The fruits which are peeled and cut up need not be pricked.

43

Place the prepared fruits in sufficient boiling water to cover them and cook gently until just tender. Overcooking spoils the shape and texture, while undercooking results in slow penetration of the syrup and causes dark colour and toughness. Tough fruits such as apricots may take 10–15 minutes, whereas soft ones need only 2–4 minutes.

Canned fruits Use good quality fruit. Pineapple chunks or small rings, plums, sliced and halved peaches and halved apricots are all suitable.

The syrup Granulated sugar is generally recommended for the preparation of the syrup. Part of the sugar may be replaced by glucose. The chart which follows gives full details of the proportion of sugar to liquid at the different stages.

Processing chart for candied fruit
Using 450 g (1 lb) prepared fruit (see notes on page 43)

Notes
Amount of syrup If the syrup is not sufficient to cover the fruit, make up more in the same strength, but remember that the amount of sugar to be added later must be increased accordingly. For example, if you increase the amount used for fresh fruit to 400 ml ($\frac{3}{4}$ pint) juice and 250 g (9 oz) sugar, on Day 2 you will have to add 75 g (3 oz) sugar and on Day 8 add 125 g ($4\frac{1}{2}$ oz) sugar.

FRESH FRUIT

Day	Syrup	Soak for	Day	Syrup	Soak for
1	Drain 300 ml ($\frac{1}{2}$ pt) cooking liquid from fruit, add 175 g (6 oz) sugar (or 50 g (2 oz) sugar and 100 g (4 oz) glucose), dissolve, bring to boil and pour over fruit.	24 hrs	6	Repeat Day 2	24 hrs
			7	Repeat Day 2	24 hrs
			8	Repeat Day 2, using a further 75 g (3 oz) sugar.	48 hrs
2	Drain off syrup, add 50 g (2 oz) sugar, dissolve, bring to boil and pour over fruit.	24 hrs	9	–	
			10	Repeat Day 8	4 days
			11	–	–
3	Repeat Day 2	24 hrs	12	–	–
4	Repeat Day 2	24 hrs	13	–	–
5	Repeat Day 2	24 hrs	14	Dry as for canned fruit	–

Soaking time It is important that the fruit should soak for a full 24 hours (or as specified) before the next lot of sugar is added.

Days 5, 7, 8, 10 When the added sugar is increased to 75 g (3 oz) first dissolve the sugar, then add the fruit and boil it in the syrup for 3–4 minutes.

Day 11 or 14 Once the syrup has reached the consistency of honey, the fruit may be left to soak for as little as 3 days or up to 2–3 weeks, according to how sweet you like the candied fruit to be.

Finishing the candied fruit
When the fruits are thoroughly dried, pack them in cardboard or wooden boxes, between layers of waxed paper, or give them one of the following finishes:

Crystallised finish Take the pieces of candied fruit and dip each quickly into boiling water; drain off excess moisture, then roll each piece in caster sugar.

Glacé finish Prepare a fresh syrup, using 450 g (1 lb) sugar and 150 ml ($\frac{1}{4}$ pint) water, bring to the boil and boil for 1 minute. Pour a little of the syrup into a cup. Dip the candied fruit into boiling water for 20 seconds, then dip one piece at a time into the syrup in the cup, using a skewer. Place the fruit on a wire rack to dry. Cover the rest of the syrup in the pan with a damp cloth and keep it warm (a double pan is useful for this purpose.) As the syrup in the cup becomes cloudy, replace it with fresh syrup from the pan.

CANNED FRUIT

Day	Syrup	Soak for	Day	Syrup	Soak for
1	Drain off canning syrup and make up to 300 ml ($\frac{1}{2}$ pt); add 225 g (8 oz) sugar (or 100 g (4 oz) sugar and 100 g (4 oz) glucose), dissolve, bring to the boil and pour over fruit.	24 hrs	5	Repeat Day 2, using 75 g (3 oz) sugar.	48 hrs
2	Drain off syrup, add 50 g (2 oz) sugar, dissolve, bring to boil and pour over fruit.	24 hrs	6	–	–
3	Repeat Day 2	24 hrs	7	Repeat Day 2, using 75 g (3 oz) sugar.	4 days
4	Repeat Day 2	24 hrs	11	Dry in oven at lowest setting or cover lightly and leave in a warm place (this may take from a few hours to 2–3 days) until quite dry; turn them 2–3 times.	–

Candied peel

Orange, lemon and grapefruit peel are all suitable. Wash or scrub the fruit thoroughly, halve it and remove the pulp. Larger pieces of peel retain their moisture better, so do not cut it up. Simmer the peel in a little water for 1–2 hours until tender. (Change the water 2–3 times when cooking grapefruit peel.) Drain well. Make the liquor up to 300 ml ($\frac{1}{2}$ pint) with water. Add 225 g (8 oz) sugar, dissolve over a low heat, then bring to the boil. Add the peel and leave for 2 days.

Drain off the syrup, dissolve another 100 g (4 oz) sugar in it and simmer the peel in this syrup until semi-transparent. The peel can be left in this thick syrup for 2–3 weeks.

Drain off the syrup, place the peel on a wire rack, cover and leave to dry. Store in screw-topped jars.

Candied angelica

Pick the green shoots in April or May, drop them straight into brine – 5 g ($\frac{1}{4}$ oz) salt to 2.3 litres (4 pints) water – and leave to soak for 10 minutes, to preserve the green colour. Rinse in cold water. Cook the angelica in boiling water until quite tender – about 5–7 minutes. Drain, retaining the water, and scrape to remove the outer skin.

Using the water the angelica was boiled in, make a syrup of 175 g (6 oz) sugar to 300 ml ($\frac{1}{2}$ pint) of the juice; place the angelica in a bowl, add the syrup, cover and leave for 24 hours.

Drain off the syrup, add 50 g (2 oz) sugar to every 300 ml ($\frac{1}{2}$ pint) of the original juice and bring to the boil; pour back into the bowl over the angelica, cover and leave for 24 hours.

Repeat the process described in the last paragraph a further five times, until the syrup is of the consistency of runny honey. Boil the angelica for 2–3 minutes at the last addition of the sugar, then leave for 2 days. Dry off on a warm rack or in the oven at 121°C (250°F) mark $\frac{1}{4}$. Store in screw-top jars.

Quick method Choose tender stalks and cut into 7.5–10-cm (3–4-in) pieces. Place in a pan with sufficient water to cover, bring to the boil, simmer until tender and bright green, then dry in a cloth. Put in a pan with 450 g (1 lb) sugar to each 450 g (1 lb) of stalks, cover and leave to stand for 2 days. Bring slowly to the boil, continue to boil until the angelica is clear and green, then put in a colander to drain. Toss the stalks in caster sugar and let them dry off in the oven at 121°C (250°F) mark $\frac{1}{4}$ before storing.

Chestnuts in syrup

225 g (8 oz) granulated sugar
225 g (8 oz) glucose or dextrose
180 ml (¼ pint plus 2 tbsp) water
350 g (12 oz) whole chestnuts, peeled and skinned
  (weight after preparation) or 350 g (12 oz) canned
  chestnuts, drained
vanilla essence

Put the granulated sugar, glucose or dextrose and water into a saucepan large enough to hold the chestnuts and heat gently until the sugars are dissolved; bring to the boil. Remove from the heat, add the chestnuts and bring to the boil again. Remove from the heat, cover and leave overnight, preferably in a warm place.

The next day, re-boil the chestnuts and syrup in the pan, without the lid; remove from the heat, cover and again leave standing overnight.

On the third day, add 6–8 drops of vanilla essence and repeat the boiling process. Warm some 450-g (1-lb) bottling jars in the oven, fill with the chestnuts and cover with syrup. Seal the jars and test that they are airtight by removing the screw-band or clip and trying to lift the jar by the cap or disc. If this holds firm it shows that a vacuum has been formed as the jars have cooled and they are hermetically sealed.

Note This recipe gives a delicious result, but the chestnuts are not exactly like commercially prepared Marrons Glacés, which cannot be reproduced under home conditions.

Novelties for Novice Cooks

Sweets for children to make – and some novelties to make for them

The recipes in this chapter will appeal to children today as they have appealed to children for generations. Toffee apples with a crisp creamy toffee, lollipops with a real fruit taste and golden buttery popcorn are but a few of them.

Some of the recipes can be made without help, even by quite young children, but recipes involving syrup boiling or toffee making, where high temperatures are involved, should always be supervised by an adult.

If they are not gobbled up as soon as they are cooled and set, they make impressive gifts for birthdays or Christmas and are ideal for selling at school fairs and bazaars and at garden fêtes. Make sure that they are attractively (yet inexpensively) wrapped with cellophane and tied with ribbons and they will sit proudly on any sweet stall. The more personal the finish, the more appealing they will be (see pages 111–125 for ideas).

If the children you know turn out to be indefatigable sweet makers, you may like to widen the net and select some of the simpler uncooked fondants and marzipans from the appropriate chapters.

Uncooked nutty chocolate fudge

Novice cooks will want to sample their efforts without delay, but if restraint is possible, this fudge is even more delicious a day or two after making.

225 g (8 oz) plain chocolate
100 g (4 oz) butter
1 egg, beaten
450 g (1 lb) caster sugar
30 ml (2 level tbsp) condensed milk
5 ml (1 tsp) vanilla essence
50 g (2 oz) walnuts, finely chopped

Grease an 18-cm (7-in) square tin. Melt the chocolate and butter together in a bowl over hot water. Mix the egg, sugar, condensed milk and vanilla essence together, then blend in the chocolate mixture. Stir in the nuts, then turn the mixture into the greased tin. Chill in the refrigerator for several hours. Cut into squares when set.
Makes about 800 g (1¾ lb)

Refrigerator nut fudge

50 g (2 oz) plain chocolate
175 g (6 oz) cream cheese
15 ml (1 tbsp) single cream
450 g (1 lb) icing sugar, sifted
100 g (4 oz) shelled nuts, coarsely chopped
pinch salt
2.5 ml ($\frac{1}{2}$ tsp) vanilla essence

Grease an 18-cm (7-in) square tin. Melt the chocolate in a bowl over hot water. Meanwhile beat the cream cheese with the cream until smooth, then add the icing sugar.

Pour the melted chocolate into the cheese mixture, stirring well, and add the nuts, salt and vanilla essence. Mix well, pour into the greased tin and press down firmly. Chill in the refrigerator for several hours and mark into squares when almost set.

Makes about 800 g (1$\frac{3}{4}$ lb)

Refrigerator fruit caramels

100 g (4 oz) stoned dates, chopped
100 g (4 oz) figs, chopped
175 g (6 oz) seedless raisins
175 g (6 oz) candied lemon or orange peel, chopped
100 g (4 oz) shelled nuts, chopped
15 ml (1 tbsp) lemon juice
10 ml (2 level tsp) golden syrup (optional)
desiccated coconut to coat

Grease a 20.5 × 15-cm (8 × 6-in) tin. Mix all the fruits and nuts together and add the lemon juice and the golden syrup (if used). Pack into the tin and leave in the refrigerator for several hours. Cut in small squares and roll these in fine desiccated coconut. Place in paper cases.

Makes about 700 g (1$\frac{1}{2}$ lb)

American raisin candy

350 g (12 oz) preserving sugar
60–90 ml (4–6 tbsp) water
175 g (6 oz) seedless raisins, chopped
50 g (2 oz) blanched almonds, chopped

Oil or butter an 18-cm (7-in) square tin. Heat the sugar and water gently in a heavy-based saucepan, tapping the lumps with a spatula, but without stirring, until the mixture becomes a golden brown syrup. Stir in the raisins and nuts and turn the mixture into the tin. When it is beginning to set, mark and cut into squares.

Makes about 450 g (1 lb)

Chocolate crispies

Illustrated in colour between pages 56, 57

This simple but delicious recipe can be varied by using other breakfast cereals.

100 g (4 oz) plain chocolate
50 g (2 oz) cornflakes

Cut up the chocolate and melt it in a bowl over a pan of hot water. When it has just melted, stir in the cornflakes and use a teaspoon to place the mixture in small heaps on a sheet of greaseproof paper. Allow to set.
Makes about 175 g (6 oz)

Marzipan animals

Illustrated in colour between pages 56, 57

As long as an adult helps with boiling the marzipan, or makes it up in advance, children can be left to supply the necessary imagination for this marzipan modelling.

Make 450–900 g (1–2 lb) boiled marzipan (*see page 29*) and divide into 75-g (3-oz) pieces. Divide each piece again roughly into two – one third for the head and two thirds for the body.

Shape little *cats* by forming the body piece into a neat oblong, making a small cut at one side to separate the tail. Shape the head, and for extra firmness, stick it on with a little melted chocolate; leave to dry out in a warm place for a few hours, then decorate with eyes, nose and whiskers. (Use tiny chocolate buttons or silver balls, and clean pastry brush bristles for whiskers.)

For marzipan *dogs*, mould the body into a sausage shape and with a sharp knife make three cuts – one in the centre at one end of the roll to mark the front legs and two equally spaced at the other end to separate the back legs and tail. Fold the back legs under, pointing forwards in a sitting position, and leave the tail

Steps in shaping a marzipan cat

and front legs straight. Make a cube-shaped head and mould ears and muzzle, snipping the sides of the muzzle for whiskers. Pipe in white eyes and a pink tongue, using icing sugar blended with a little water, and roll balls of marzipan for the eyeballs and nose.

Tint the marzipan pink to make *pigs*, using split almonds for feet and mounting them on a flat piece of green-tinted marzipan.

Try your hand at as many different animals as you can. It is easy to make them realistic – in fact they might be too convincing to eat!

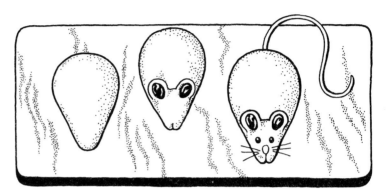

Steps in shaping a sugar mouse

Sugar mice   *Illustrated in colour between pages 56, 57*

As with the previous recipe, once the fondant has been boiled (see page 20) children can be left to make their own mice.

You will need about 50 g (2 oz) fondant for each mouse. For white mice, about one eighth of the fondant should be coloured pink or brown: for pink mice, add food colouring to the bulk of the fondant and leave about one eighth white. Shape the large quantity of fondant into a pear-shaped piece and place on a baking sheet. Gently mould the ears and use the contrasting fondant to colour the inside part. Fix a small length of white string at the wide end of each mouse to represent the tail and use clean pastry brush bristles for whiskers. Roll small balls of the contrasting fondant for the eyes and nose, or else stick on tiny chocolate buttons or small pieces of glacé cherry.

Coconut ice bars   *Illustrated in colour on the jacket*

450 g (1 lb) granulated sugar
150 ml (¼ pint) milk
150 g (5 oz) desiccated coconut
few drops of red food colouring

Oil or butter a 20.5 × 15-cm (8 × 6-in) tin. Dissolve the sugar in

53

the milk in a heavy saucepan over a low heat. Bring to the boil and boil gently for about 10 minutes, or until a temperature of 116°C (240°F) (soft ball stage) is reached.

Remove from the heat and stir in the coconut. Pour half The mixture quickly into the tin. Add a few drops of food colouring to the second half and pour quickly over the first layer. Leave until half set, mark into bars and cut or break when cold. *Makes about 550 g (1¼ lb)*

Plain lollipops

225 g (8 oz) granulated sugar
100 g (4 oz) golden syrup
150 ml (¼ pint) water
lollipop sticks

Oil a marble or enamel surface. In a heavy-based saucepan, heat all the ingredients gently until the sugar has dissolved. Bring to the boil and boil to 130°C (265°F) (hard ball stage).

Using a dessertspoon, pour a little of the syrup on to the oiled surface so that it forms rounds. Put a lollipop stick into each round while it is still soft, then pour on a little more syrup to cover the stick. Leave the lollipops to set hard, then carefully lift them from the slab and wrap them in cellophane.

Fruity lollipops

Illustrated in colour between pages 56, 57

This recipe tells you how to make four different flavours of lollipop from one quantity of syrup; it is of course possible, though not so colourful, to make them all the same.

450 g (1 lb) granulated sugar
15 ml (1 level tbsp) powdered glucose
150 ml (¼ pint) water
various food colourings and flavourings
lollipop sticks

Oil a marble or enamel surface. Dissolve the sugar and glucose in the water in a heavy-based saucepan, heating very gently. Pour this syrup into a measuring jug.

Return a quarter of the syrup to the pan, colour it pink and bring to the boil. Boil to 130°C (265°F) (hard ball stage), remove from the heat and add a few drops of raspberry flavouring. Using a dessertspoon, pour a little of the syrup on to the oiled surface so that it forms rounds. Put a lollipop stick into each round while it is still soft, then pour on a little more syrup to cover the stick. Leave the lollipops to set hard, then carefully lift them from the slab and wrap in cellophane.

Fruity lollipops: making sure the stick is covered by pouring over a little more syrup

Repeat three times with the remaining syrup, boiling it up a quarter at a time and adding suitable combinations of colourings and flavourings, for example green colouring with peppermint; yellow with lemon essence.

Lollipop surprises

Illustrated in colour between pages 56, 57

350 g (12 oz) golden syrup
juice of 2 lemons
red or green food colouring (optional)
dates or figs, stoned
lollipop sticks

Boil the syrup and the lemon juice to 130°C (265°F) (hard ball stage). Remove from the heat and add a few drops of colouring if liked. Put a whole date or a fig on a stick and dip it into the syrup, then twirl round to coat the fruit thoroughly. Lay the lollipop on a buttered baking sheet to harden and repeat with the remaining fruit.

Toffee apples   *Illustrated in colour overleaf*

450 g (1 lb) demerara sugar
50 g (2 oz) butter
10 ml (2 tsp) vinegar
150 ml (¼ pint) water
15 ml (1 level tbsp) golden syrup
6–8 medium sized apples and the same number of
    wooden sticks

Heat the sugar, butter, vinegar, water and syrup gently in a heavy-based saucepan. When the sugar has dissolved, boil rapidly for 5 minutes until the temperature reaches 143°C (290°F) (soft crack stage).

Wipe the apples and push the sticks into the cores. Dip the apples into the toffee, twirl around for few seconds to allow excess toffee to drip off, then leave to cool and set on a buttered baking sheet or waxed paper.

Edinburgh rock

450 g (1 lb) granulated sugar
300 ml (½ pint) water
pinch cream of tartar
food colourings
flavourings
icing sugar

Grease a marble or enamel slab. Heat the sugar and water gently in a heavy-based saucepan, stirring all the time. When the sugar is dissolved, add the cream of tartar, bring to the boil and boil to 127°C (260°F) (hard ball stage).

Pour the mixture on to the greased slab and allow it to cool for a few minutes, then, using a palette knife, turn the sides to the middle until it is cool enough to handle. Divide it into two portions and knead in a suitable colouring and flavouring to each portion.

Dip the fingers in icing sugar and gently pull one portion, without twisting it, until it becomes dull. Pull it to a rope and lay it on waxed paper. Repeat with the other portion. When the rock is nearly set, cut into 10-cm (4-in) strips; leave for 24 hours in a warm room, until powdery and soft.
Makes about 450 g (1 lb)

Popcorn   *Illustrated in colour overleaf*

Corn for popping can be bought in packets, which also include the fat in which it is to be cooked. Heat the fat in a large heavy-

Opposite Crèmes de menthe (page 39), Orange and lemon slices (*page 42*)

Overleaf Fruity lollipops (*page 54*), Toffee apples (*above*), Chocolate crispies, Marzipan animals (*page 52*), Sugar mice (*page 53*), Home-made marshmallow (*page 57*), Lollipop surprises (*page 55*), plain and buttered Popcorn (*above and page 57*)

based saucepan. When the fat is really hot, put in a sparse layer of corn, put the lid on the pan and keep shaking the pan over a good heat. Do not remove the lid until all the 'popping' has stopped.

Buttered popcorn

Melt equal quantities of butter and golden syrup in a saucepan over a gentle heat and turn some cooked popcorn in the mixture until it is evenly coated.

Coloured sweet popcorn

Make a thin glacé icing, divide into three and add food colouring to make one portion pink, one green and one yellow, making the colours fairly strong. Add some cooked popcorn to the coloured icing, stir round to coat it thoroughly, then place on a wire tray to drain. The icing will go quite hard and crisp with exposure to the air.

Home-made marshmallow

Illustrated in colour between pages 56, 57

275 g (10 oz) granulated sugar
10 ml (2 level tsp) powdered glucose
300 ml ($\frac{1}{2}$ pint) tepid water
20 g ($\frac{3}{4}$ oz) powdered gelatine
15–30 ml (1–2 tbsp) orangeflower water
1 egg white, stiffly beaten
icing sugar

Line a 20.5 × 15-cm (8 × 6-in) tin with greaseproof paper and dredge with icing sugar. In a heavy-based saucepan, dissolve the sugar and glucose in 150 ml ($\frac{1}{4}$ pint) of the water and boil to 127°C (260°F) (hard ball stage). Meanwhile, dissolve the gelatine in the remaining 150 ml ($\frac{1}{4}$ pint) water and keep it warm.

Pour the gelatine on to the boiling syrup, whisking all the time. Add the orangeflower water then the egg white and continue whisking until the mixture is thick and stiff – it may take as long as 20 minutes. While still liquid, pour it into the prepared tin and leave to set. Cut it up with scissors, or into 2.5-cm (1-in) rounds, roll in icing sugar and leave to dry for about 24 hours.
Makes about 350 g (12 oz)

Note Gum arabic may be substituted for the gelatine in this recipe.

Coffee truffles (*page 109*), Chocolate rum truffles (*page 107*), Chocolate orange liqueur truffles, Parisian truffles, Mocha truffles (*page 108*)

Marshmallow delight

Follow the previous recipe for Home-made marshmallow, adding 25 g (1 oz) chopped toasted almonds and 25 g (1 oz) chopped glacé cherries during the beating.

Lemon marshmallow

Use the basic marshmallow recipe but substitute 2.5 ml ($\frac{1}{2}$ tsp) lemon essence for the orangeflower water and add a few drops of yellow food colouring.

Peppermint marshmallow

Substitute 2.5 ml ($\frac{1}{2}$ tsp) peppermint essence (not oil of peppermint) for the orangeflower water in the basic marshmallow recipe and add a few drops of green food colouring.

Pretty Petits Fours

An assortment of rich little goodies to serve with coffee after dinner

Petits fours are the delicious, rich little sweets and biscuits that are served with coffee after dinner.

Traditional petits fours always include little iced cakes made from a Genoese sponge mixture cut into small shapes – triangles, squares, rounds or shapes cut with small fancy cutters. They are coated with apricot jam and then covered with fondant, marzipan or glacé icing. They may be decorated with nuts, glacé fruits, crystallised flower petals, etc.

Marzipan based sweets are ideal, and macaroon and meringue mixtures may be piped into fancy shapes, cooked then decorated with small pieces of glacé cherry or nuts or dipped in chocolate. Caramelled fruits and sugared nuts add to the mouthwatering and irresistible display.

Almost any small rich sweets can be included and as much variety as possible should be offered. A good selection should be colourful and varied in shape, texture and type. Select suitable truffles, chocolates and fondants from the appropriate chapters.

Storage time for petits fours will vary according to type, but in general they are best stored in airtight tins for fairly short periods.

Caramelled fruits

Illustrated in colour on the jacket

about 450 g (1 lb) mixed prepared fruit
225 g (8 oz) preserving sugar
60 ml (4 tbsp) water
5 ml (1 level tsp) powdered glucose
large pinch cream of tartar

Suitable fruits are orange or mandarin segments, small pieces of pineapple, black or white grapes, cherries or strawberries. Select only perfect fruit without bruises or defects. Wash and dry it carefully and drain canned fruit thoroughly. Skewer each piece of fruit on a fork or cocktail stick.

Make a syrup of the sugar and water in a small, deep, heavy-based saucepan. When the sugar has dissolved, add the glucose and cream of tartar. Boil gently until it is golden brown and has reached a temperature of 143°C (290°F) (soft crack stage).

Dip the prepared fruit, one piece at a time, into the syrup.

Drain well by tapping the fork gently on the edge of the saucepan and place neatly on an oiled slab or plate, without touching, until quite dry. Then place in paper cases.

Chocolate marzipan almonds

225 g (8 oz) marzipan
40 g (1½ oz) whole blanched almonds
75 g (3 oz) plain or milk chocolate

Knead the marzipan until smooth and divide into the same number of pieces as there are almonds. Enclose each almond completely in a piece of the marzipan.

Break up the chocolate into small pieces and place in a bowl over a saucepan of hot water. Heat gently until the chocolate has melted, stirring occasionally, making sure that the water is not allowed to boil. Remove the pan from the heat.

Dip each marzipan-covered almond into the melted chocolate using a small fork or wooden cocktail stick. Place on waxed or greaseproof paper and leave in a cool place until the chocolate has hardened, then transfer the sweets to paper cases.

Makes about 30

Almond stars

Illustrated in colour facing page 65

2 egg whites
150 g (5 oz) ground almonds
75 g (3 oz) caster sugar
few drops of almond essence
angelica or glacé cherries to decorate

Line two baking sheets with greaseproof paper. Whisk the egg whites until they are stiff and use a tablespoon to fold in the almonds, sugar and essence.

Using a large star vegetable nozzle, pipe stars, quite close together, on to the lined baking sheets.

Decorate with a piece of angelica or glacé cherry and bake in the oven at 150°C (300°F) mark 2 for 15–20 minutes until just beginning to colour.
Makes about 24

Almond button petits fours

Illustrated in colour facing page 65

75 g (3 oz) ground almonds
175 g (6 oz) granulated sugar
2 egg whites
25 g (1 oz) blanched almonds, halved

Line a baking sheet with rice or waxed paper. Place the ground almonds and sugar in a mixing bowl and stir until well blended. Add the egg whites and stir until the mixture is firm.

Using an icing bag fitted with a plain 0.5-cm ($\frac{1}{4}$-in) nozzle, pipe small rounds of mixture, about the size of a ten pence piece, on to the lined baking sheet. Top each round with half a blanched almond. Bake in the oven at 190°C (375°F) mark 5 for 7–10 minutes until just beginning to colour.
Makes about 30

Chocolate cups

Illustrated in colour facing page 96

150 g (5 oz) plain chocolate
100 g (4 oz) glacé cherries, chopped
15 ml (1 tbsp) rum
1 egg yolk, beaten
10 ml (2 level tsp) icing sugar, sifted

Place 32 paper petits fours cases on a baking sheet, one inside another, to make 16 cases of double thickness. Melt 125 g ($4\frac{1}{2}$ oz) chocolate in a bowl over a saucepan of hot water. Spoon some chocolate into each case and run it round to coat; leave to set. Coat with more chocolate; let excess drip off by upturning the

cases on a baking sheet. Chill the cases and, meanwhile, marinade the cherries in the rum for 1 hour.

Peel off the outer layers of paper, then gently pull away the inner paper cases. Melt the remaining chocolate and when cool, stir in the rum from the cherries, egg yolk and icing sugar. Put the cherries into the chocolate cases and pipe in the chocolate cream, using a small star nozzle.

Makes about 16

Note As an alternative to peeling off the paper cases, make and serve the chocolate cups in brightly coloured foil cases.

Chocolate and hazelnut petits fours

75 g (3 oz) ground almonds
175 g (6 oz) granulated sugar
45 ml (3 level tbsp) drinking chocolate or cocoa powder
2 egg whites
25 g (1 oz) whole hazelnuts, skinned and halved
50 g (2 oz) plain chocolate

Line a baking sheet with non-stick paper. Place the ground almonds, sugar and drinking chocolate or cocoa powder in a mixing bowl and stir until well blended. Add the egg whites and

63

stir until the mixture is firm. Using an icing bag fitted with a plain 0.5-cm ($\frac{1}{4}$-in) nozzle, pipe 5-cm (2-in) lengths, well spaced, on to the lined baking sheet. Place half a hazelnut in the centre of each bar. Bake in the oven at 190°C (375°F) mark 5 for 5–7 minutes until firm to the touch. Cool.

Place the chocolate in a small basin over a pan of water and heat gently, without boiling, until the chocolate has melted. Dip both ends of each bar into the chocolate and leave to dry.

Makes about 30

Chocolate boxes

genoese sponge (*see page 67*)
225 g (8 oz) plain chocolate
50 g (2 oz) butter
75 g (3 oz) icing sugar, sifted
30 ml (2 level tbsp) cocoa powder

Make up the genoese sponge on page 67 and bake in a greased and lined 20.5-cm (8-in) square tin at 190°C (375°F) mark 5 for 20–25 minutes, until risen and golden brown. Turn out and leave to cool. Cut the sponge into 2.5-cm (1-in) cubes.

Break up the chocolate and place in a small bowl over a pan of water and heat gently until melted. Pour on to a sheet of greaseproof paper and leave until set. Cut into 2.5-cm (1-in) squares.

Cream the butter, icing sugar and cocoa powder together until smooth and creamy. Spoon into a greaseproof paper icing bag fitted with a rosette nozzle. Pipe a little butter cream on the back of each piece of chocolate and push on to the four sides of each

cube of sponge. Pipe a zig zag border along one top edge and place a chocolate square on top as the lid. Continue with the remaining sponge and chocolate squares. Place in paper cases.
Makes 64

Tutti frutti petits fours

50 g (2 oz) ground almonds
100 g (4 oz) granulated sugar
15 g ($\frac{1}{2}$ oz) angelica
25 g (1 oz) glacé cherries
1 egg white
100 g (4 oz) plain chocolate

Place the ground almonds and sugar in a mixing bowl and stir until well blended. Wash the angelica and cherries in warm water, dry on kitchen paper towel and chop. Stir into the ground almond mixture with the egg white and mix until firm. Turn on to a board dusted with icing sugar and roll into a log about 4 cm ($1\frac{1}{2}$ in) in diameter.

Place the chocolate in a small bowl over a pan of water and heat gently, without boiling, until the chocolate has melted. Spoon over the marzipan log, making sure it is completely covered. Leave to dry and set. Cut into 0.5–1-cm ($\frac{1}{4}$–$\frac{1}{2}$-in) slices.
Makes about 25

Meringue petits fours

Illustrated in colour opposite

2 egg whites
125 g (4 oz) icing sugar
10–15 ml (2–3 tsp) coffee essence
glacé cherries to decorate
angelica to decorate

Line a baking sheet with non-stick paper. Place the egg whites and sugar in a mixing bowl over a pan of hot water and whisk until the mixture is very thick and stands in peaks. Remove the bowl from the heat. Place half the mixture in an icing bag fitted with a plain 1-cm ($\frac{1}{2}$-in) nozzle and pipe small rounds of the mixture, about 2.5 cm (1 in) in diameter, on the lined baking sheet. Add the coffee essence to the remaining mixture and pipe an equal number of rounds. Reserve any uncooked meringue mixture. Bake in the oven at 170°C (325°F) mark 3 for 10–15 minutes until set but not coloured. Cool. Use a little uncooked meringue mixture to sandwich one white and one coffee meringue together. Decorate each with a little piece of glacé cherry and angelica.
Makes about 25

Almond stars, Almond button petits fours (*page 62*), Almond meringue petits fours (*page 68*), Meringue petits fours (*above*)

Mandarin barquettes

100 g (4 oz) plain flour
pinch salt
50 g (2 oz) butter
25 g (1 oz) caster sugar
1 egg yolk
1.25 ml ($\frac{1}{4}$ tsp) vanilla essence
312-g (11-oz) can mandarin oranges
30 ml (2 tbsp) apricot jam
15 ml (1 tbsp) water
pistachio nuts, blanched and halved, or glacé cherries, halved, to decorate

Heat the oven to 180°C (350°F) mark 4. Sift the flour and salt into a bowl, rub in the fat and stir in the sugar, egg yolk and vanilla essence. Knead gently and roll out to 0.5 cm ($\frac{1}{4}$ in) thick between sheets of waxed paper.

Place some barquette moulds close together on a baking sheet and cover with the pastry. Move the rolling pin over the top to cut out the shapes, then push the pastry gently down into each mould and use a finger to mould it up the sides. Prick the pastry with a fork and bake in the oven for about 15 minutes. Cool slightly, and carefully remove from the moulds.

Drain the fruit and put 3 mandarin segments in each case. Heat the jam and water together in a small pan; sieve, and brush over the fruit. Decorate.
Makes about 18

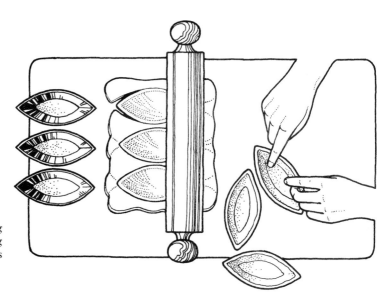

Mandarin barquettes: cutting out boat shapes and moulding pastry up the sides of the tins

Iced petits fours

For the genoese sponge
25 g (1 oz) butter
40 g (1½ oz) plain flour
15 g (½ oz) cornflour
2 eggs
50 g (2 oz) caster sugar
apricot jam
50 g (2 oz) almond paste

For the decoration
225 g (8 oz) icing sugar, sifted
food colourings
crystallised flowers, grated chocolate, nuts

For the sponge, grease and line a 20.5-cm (8-in) square tin. Heat the butter gently until it is melted and leave to cool until the sediment has settled. Sift the flour and cornflour together on to a plate. Whisk the eggs and sugar together in a mixing bowl over a pan of hot water until thick and creamy. Remove from the heat and whisk until cool. Re-sift half the flour and cornflour over the surface of the egg mixture and fold in carefully with a metal spoon. Pour half the melted butter around the edge of the mixture and carefully fold in with the metal spoon. Repeat using the remaining flour and butter. Pour the mixture into the prepared tin and bake in the oven at 190°C (375°F) mark 5 for 20–25 minutes until risen and golden brown. Turn out and cool on a wire rack.

When the cake is cold, cut into shapes about 3.5 cm (1½ in) in size, e.g. rounds, oblongs, squares, diamonds, triangles, crescents. Heat the apricot jam gently, adding a little water if the jam is very thick. Brush each petit four with the apricot glaze. Divide the almond paste and add a ball or roll of almond paste to the top of each petit four.

For the decoration, blend the icing sugar with a little water to make glacé icing. Divide the icing and colour yellow, pink, peach, coffee and chocolate, and leave some white. Spoon the icing over the petits fours, making sure each one is completely covered. Decorate with mimosa balls, glacé cherries, grated chocolate, nuts or crystallised flowers. Leave to set and place in paper cases.
Makes 25–30

Variation
Coat the petits fours in melted boiled fondant (*see page 20*). Decorate and leave to set as above.

Almond meringue petits fours

Illustrated in colour facing page 65

2 egg whites
125 g (4 oz) icing sugar
50 g (2 oz) blanched almonds, chopped
few drops of pink food colouring

Grease two baking sheets. Place the egg whites and sugar in a mixing bowl over a pan of hot water and whisk until the mixture is very thick and stands in peaks. Remove the bowl from the heat and fold in the chopped almonds.

Divide the mixture in half and colour one half pale pink. Spoon small mounds of mixture on to the baking sheets. Bake in the oven at 170°C (325°F) mark 3 for 10–15 minutes until set but not coloured. Cool.

Makes about 30

A Fondness for Fudge

Cooked fudges

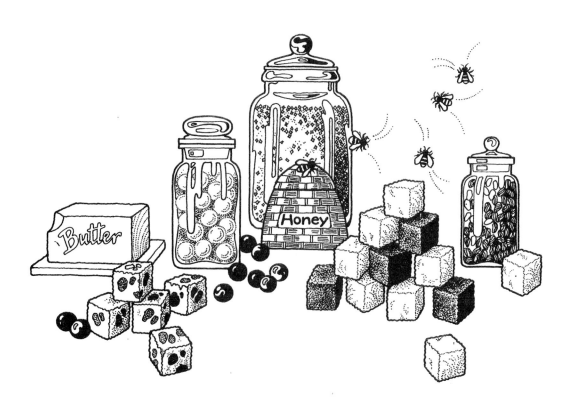

It is easy to see why melt-in-the-mouth fudges are so popular: they are also quite simple to make. Fudge can be flavoured with such things as chocolate, coffee, nuts or glacé fruits.

Cooked fudge is made from sugar, butter and milk or cream that is gently heated and then boiled to the required temperature. Either caster or granulated sugar may be used, but caster sugar dissolves more easily. Fudge mixtures, unlike most toffees, have to be stirred constantly during cooking otherwise they may stick to the bottom of the pan and burn. When the required temperature is reached, the mixture is beaten with a wooden spoon to give the characteristic creamy texture.

Immediately the fudge begins to thicken it should be poured into the prepared tins. Mark it into squares just before it begins to set. A knife dipped in hot water makes cutting easier.

To store fudge after cutting, place it between sheets of waxed paper and then in an airtight tin. Cooked fudges keep fairly well, but if you are making any of the uncooked fudges in the 'Novice' chapter, eat them up within 24 hours.

Vanilla fudge

450 g (1 lb) granulated sugar
50 g (2 oz) butter
150 ml (¼ pint) evaporated milk
150 ml (¼ pint) milk
few drops of vanilla essence

Grease a 15-cm (6-in) square tin. In a large heavy-based saucepan gently heat the sugar, butter and milks until the sugar has dissolved and the fat melted. Bring to the boil and boil steadily to 116°C (240°F) (soft ball stage), stirring occasionally.

Remove the pan from the heat, place on a cool surface, add the essence and beat until the mixture becomes thick and creamy and 'grains' – i.e. until minute crystals form. Pour it immediately into the tin. Leave until nearly cold, then mark into squares.
Makes about 700 g (1½ lb)

Marshmallow fudge

Follow the directions for Vanilla fudge (see above) but add 225 g (8 oz) chopped marshmallows to the mixture before beating.

Coconut fudge

350 g (12 oz) granulated sugar
400 ml (¾ pint) milk
175 g (6 oz) desiccated coconut
5 ml (1 tsp) vanilla essence

Grease an 18 × 12.5-cm (7 × 5-in) tin. In a large heavy-based saucepan gently heat the sugar, milk and coconut until the sugar is dissolved, then boil steadily to 116°C (240°F) (soft ball stage), stirring all the time.

Remove the pan from the heat, add the essence and keep on stirring until the mixture becomes thick. Pour into the tin, leave until nearly set, then mark into squares with a sharp knife.
Makes about 700 g (1½ lb)

Date fudge

150 ml (¼ pint) milk
450 g (1 lb) rich brown soft sugar
75 g (3 oz) plain chocolate, grated
50 g (2 oz) butter
good pinch cream of tartar
10 ml (2 tsp) lemon juice
100 g (4 oz) stoned dates, finely chopped

Grease a 20.5 × 15-cm (8 × 6-in) tin. Put the milk, sugar, chocolate, butter and cream of tartar into a heavy-based saucepan and bring to a temperature of 116°C (240°F) (soft ball stage), stirring frequently as the mixture burns easily.

Remove from the heat. Add the lemon juice and dates and beat until thick and creamy. Pour into the tin, leave until nearly set, then mark into pieces with a sharp knife.
Makes about 700 g (1½ lb)

Raisin fudge

Replace the dates in the above recipe with 75 g (3 oz) chopped seedless raisins.

Ginger fudge

This is another, more exotic, variation on Date fudge, made by replacing the dates with 50 g (2 oz) finely chopped preserved ginger and a few drops of ginger essence.

Fruit fudge

450 g (1 lb) granulated sugar
50 g (2 oz) butter
150 ml (¼ pint) water
150 ml (¼ pint) fresh or evaporated milk
50 g (2 oz) glacé cherries, chopped
50 g (2 oz) sultanas
25 g (1 oz) angelica, chopped

Grease an 18 × 12.5-cm (7 × 5-in) tin. Gently heat the sugar, butter, water and milk in a heavy-based saucepan until the sugar dissolves, then boil steadily until a temperature of 116°C (240°F) (soft ball stage) is reached.

Remove the pan from the heat and beat the fudge very well, then add the fruit and continue beating until the mixture becomes creamy. Pour into the tin, leave until nearly set, then mark into pieces with a sharp knife.
Makes about 550 g (1¼ lb)

Soft honey fudge

100 g (4 oz) honey
450 g (1 lb) caster sugar
150 ml (¼ pint) water
1.25 ml (¼ level tsp) cream of tartar
2 egg whites

Use a round-bladed knife to lift Soft honey fudge from the tin

Grease a 30.5 × 10-cm (12 × 4-in) tin. Gently heat the honey, sugar, water and cream of tartar in a heavy-based saucepan until the sugar is dissolved. Boil until a temperature of 130°C (265°F) (hard ball stage) is reached.

72

Whisk the egg whites in a large bowl until stiff. Pour the boiling syrup slowly on to the egg whites and whisk vigorously. Continue whisking until the mixture is very thick and loses its gloss; (an electric mixer is excellent for this and saves time, although a hand whisk is quite satisfactory). Pour into the tin and leave overnight.

The next day, remove the fudge from the tin by cutting it into 2.5-cm (1-in) squares using a hot wet knife, lifting the pieces out with a round-bladed knife.

Makes about 550 g (1¼ lb)

Variation
Include 50 g (2 oz) seedless raisins, folding them in before pouring the fudge into the tin.

Orange fudge

900 g (2 lb) granulated sugar
300 ml (½ pint) evaporated milk
100 g (4 oz) butter
grated rind of ½ an orange
60 ml (4 tbsp) orange juice

Grease a 30.5 × 10-cm (12 × 4-in) or an 18-cm (7-in) square tin. Gently heat the sugar, milk and butter in a large heavy-based saucepan until the sugar has dissolved. Add the orange rind and juice, bring to the boil and boil steadily to 116°C (240°F) (soft ball stage), stirring continuously to prevent sticking.

Remove from the heat, place the pan on a cool surface and beat until thick, creamy and beginning to 'grain'. Pour into the tin and leave until nearly cold, then mark into squares; when firm, cut with a sharp knife.

Makes about 1.1 kg (2½ lb)

Variation
Substitute lemon rind and juice for the orange to make Lemon fudge.

Nut fudge

small pinch bicarbonate of soda
75 ml (5 tbsp) water
450 g (1 lb) light brown soft sugar
150 ml (¼ pint) milk
225 g (8 oz) shelled nuts, chopped

Grease a 30.5 × 10-cm (12 × 4-in) tin. In a heavy-based saucepan, dissolve the bicarbonate of soda in the water; add the sugar and milk and stir occasionally over a low heat until the sugar is dissolved. Boil to 116°C (240°F) (soft ball stage), stirring

frequently. Add the nuts and beat carefully until the mixture is thick and creamy. Pour into the tin and mark into squares with a sharp knife when nearly cold.
Makes about 700 g (1½ lb)

Orange and pineapple fudge

Illustrated in colour facing page 64

550 g (1¼ lb) caster sugar
200 ml (⅓ pint) milk
100 g (4 oz) butter
45 ml (3 tbsp) orange juice
30 ml (2 tbsp) grated orange rind
75 g (3 oz) glacé pineapple, chopped

Grease a 20.5 × 15-cm (8 × 6-in) tin. In a heavy-based saucepan, dissolve the sugar in the milk over a low heat and boil for 5 minutes. Add the butter, orange juice and rind. Stir occasionally and boil to 116°C (240°F) (soft ball stage).

Remove from the heat, add half the pineapple and beat until smooth and creamy. Pour the fudge into the tin, arrange small pieces of pineapple over the top and when the fudge is nearly cold, mark it into squares with a sharp knife.
Makes about 700 g (1½ lb)

Ginger chocolate fudge

Illustrated in colour facing page 64

50 g (2 oz) caster sugar
50 g (2 oz) cocoa powder
568 ml (1 pint) milk
10 ml (2 level tsp) powdered glucose
100 g (4 oz) butter
75 g (3 oz) crystallised ginger, chopped

Butter a 20.5 × 15-cm (8 × 6-in) tin. Blend together the sugar and cocoa in a heavy-based saucepan and add the milk. Stir over a low heat until the sugar is dissolved, then add the glucose and butter. Bring to the boil, stirring all the time, and boil gently until the temperature reaches 116°C (240°F) (soft ball stage).

Remove from the heat and place on a cool surface, then add the ginger and beat with a wooden spoon until thick and creamy. When the mixture shows signs of setting, pour it into the tin. Mark it into squares with a sharp knife when nearly cold.
Makes about 900 g (2 lb)

Creamy chocolate almond fudge

450 g (1 lb) caster sugar
300 ml (½ pint) water
1 large can condensed milk
100 g (4 oz) cooking chocolate, grated
75 g (3 oz) flaked almonds, toasted

Grease a 20.5 × 15-cm (8 × 6-in) tin, or an 18-cm (7-in) square tin. Heat the sugar and water gently in a heavy-based saucepan until the sugar dissolves. Bring the mixture to the boil, add the condensed milk and boil to a temperature of 116°C (240°F) (soft ball stage), stirring to prevent sticking.

Remove the pan from the heat and place on a cool surface. Add the chocolate and nuts and beat well until thick and creamy. Pour into the prepared tin. When almost cold, mark into squares with a sharp knife.
Makes about 800 g (1¾ lb)

Coffee walnut fudge

Illustrated in colour facing page 64

700 g (1½ lb) granulated sugar
300 ml (½ pint) evaporated milk
150 ml (¼ pint) water
100 g (4 oz) butter
25 ml (1½ level tbsp) instant coffee
50 g (2 oz) shelled walnuts, chopped

Grease a 20.5-cm (8-in) square tin. Put the sugar, milk, water and butter into a 3.4-litre (6-pint) heavy-based saucepan. Blend the coffee with 15 ml (1 tbsp) water, add to the pan and stir the mixture over a low heat until the sugar has dissolved. Boil gently to 116°C (240°F) (soft ball stage), stirring to prevent sticking.

Remove from the heat, place the pan on a cool surface, add the nuts and beat with a wooden spoon until thick, creamy and beginning to 'grain'. Pour into the tin and mark into squares with a sharp knife when nearly cold.
Makes about 900 g (2 lb)

Tutti frutti fudge

100 g (4 oz) golden syrup
25 g (1 oz) butter
75 ml (5 tbsp) condensed milk
30 ml (2 tbsp) water
25 g (1 oz) cooking chocolate
175 g (6 oz) granulated sugar
2–3 drops of vanilla essence
175 g (6 oz) prunes, or prunes and dates, stoned and chopped

Butter a 20.5 × 10-cm (8 × 4-in) tin. In a heavy-based saucepan heat the syrup, butter, milk, water and chocolate to boiling point, then boil for 2 minutes. Remove the pan from the heat, add the sugar and dissolve slowly. As soon as the sugar dissolves, bring the mixture rapidly to the boil again and continue to boil without stirring to a temperature of 116°C (240°F) (soft ball stage).

Remove from the heat and add the essence and the fruit. Beat until creamy and turn the mixture at once into the tin. Leave until almost cold then mark into squares with a sharp knife.
Makes about 450 g (1 lb)

Walnut fudge

450 g (1 lb) granulated sugar
50 g (2 oz) butter
150 ml ($\frac{1}{4}$ pint) evaporated milk
150 ml ($\frac{1}{4}$ pint) milk
25 g (1 oz) shelled walnuts, chopped
few drops of vanilla essence

Grease a 20.5 × 15-cm (8 × 6-in) tin. In a heavy-based saucepan gently heat the sugar, butter and milks until the sugar dissolves and the butter melts. Bring to the boil and boil steadily to 116°C (240°F) (soft ball stage), stirring occasionally.

Remove from heat, place on a cool surface and add the nuts and vanilla essence. Beat until the mixture becomes thick and creamy and 'grains'. Quickly pour into the tin and mark into squares. Alternatively, leave the fudge until cool, shape into balls and roll in chocolate vermicelli.
Makes about 700 g (1$\frac{1}{2}$ lb)

Nut and raisin fudge

200 ml ($\frac{1}{3}$ pint) milk
450 g (1 lb) rich brown soft sugar
50 g (2 oz) cooking chocolate, grated
40 g (1$\frac{1}{2}$ oz) butter
pinch cream of tartar
50 g (2 oz) seedless raisins, chopped
25 g (1 oz) shelled nuts, chopped

Grease a 20.5 × 15-cm (8 × 6-in) tin. In a heavy-based saucepan bring the milk, sugar, chocolate, butter and cream of tartar slowly to the boil, then cook, stirring frequently, until a temperature of 116°C (240°F) is reached. Remove from the heat and add the raisins and nuts. Beat the fudge until it is creamy then pour into the tin. When nearly set mark into squares.
Makes about 700 g (1$\frac{1}{2}$ lb)

76

Nut and cherry fudge

Illustrated in colour facing page 64

450 g (1 lb) granulated sugar
300 ml (½ pint) evaporated or fresh milk
50 g (2 oz) butter
50 g (2 oz) blanched almonds, toasted and chopped
100 g (4 oz) glacé cherries, roughly chopped

Grease a 20.5 × 15-cm (8 × 6-in) tin. Dissolve the sugar in the milk in a heavy-based saucepan. Bring to the boil, add the butter and boil to 116°C (240°F) (soft ball stage), stirring all the time. Remove from the heat, add the nuts and cherries and beat until creamy. Pour into the tin and even the surface. Mark into squares when almost set.
Makes about 700 g (1½ lb)

Chocolate fudge

Illustrated in colour facing page 64

450 g (1 lb) granulated sugar
150 ml (¼ pint) milk
150 g (5 oz) butter
150 g (5 oz) plain chocolate
50 g (2 oz) honey

Grease a 20.5 × 15-cm (8 × 6-in) tin. Heat all the ingredients gently in a large heavy-based saucepan, stirring until the sugar has dissolved. Bring to the boil and boil to 116°C (240°F) (soft ball stage).

Remove from the heat, stand the pan on a cool surface for 5 minutes, then beat the mixture until thick, creamy and beginning to 'grain'. Pour into the tin, mark into squares with a sharp knife and cut when cold.
Makes about 800 g (1¾ lb)

Peppermint ice

450 g (1 lb) granulated sugar
150 ml (¼ pint) milk
5 ml (1 tsp) peppermint essence
few drops of green food colouring (optional)

Have ready a 20.5 × 15-cm (8 × 6-in) tin. Put the sugar and milk into a heavy-based saucepan and stir until they come to the boil. Stir occasionally until a temperature of 118°C (245°F) (hard ball stage) is reached. Remove the mixture from the heat, add peppermint essence and stir evenly until it begins to turn thick. Stir in a little green food colouring if liked.

Dampen the inside of the tin and pour the mixture into this. Leave until nearly cold then cut into neat pieces of equal size.
Makes about 450 g (1 lb)

Christmas fudge

300 ml ($\frac{1}{2}$ pint) milk
800 g ($1\frac{3}{4}$ lb) granulated sugar
100 g (4 oz) butter
10 ml (2 tsp) vanilla essence
15 g ($\frac{1}{2}$ oz) currants
15 g ($\frac{1}{2}$ oz) glacé cherries, chopped
15 g ($\frac{1}{2}$ oz) blanched almonds, chopped
15 g ($\frac{1}{2}$ oz) walnuts, chopped
15 g ($\frac{1}{2}$ oz) candied angelica, chopped

Grease an 18-cm (7-in) square tin. Pour the milk into a heavy-based saucepan and bring slowly to the boil. Add the sugar and butter and heat slowly, stirring all the time, until the sugar dissolves and butter melts.

Bring the mixture to the boil, cover the pan and boil for 2 minutes. Uncover and continue to boil steadily to 116°C (240°F) (soft ball stage), stirring occasionally.

Remove the pan from the heat. Stir in the vanilla essence, fruit, nuts and angelica and leave to cool for 5 minutes. Beat the fudge until it just begins to lose its gloss and is thick and creamy. Pour it into the tin. Mark it into squares when cool and cut up with a sharp knife when set.
Makes about 1.1 kg (2$\frac{1}{2}$ lb)

Turn a Fine Toffee

Toffees, including pulled toffee, brittles and caramels

Delicious toffees – hard or soft, chewy or brittle – can success-fully be made in your very own kitchen. They do, however, need care and accuracy.

The temperatures to which toffee needs to be boiled vary according to type, and care must be taken to prevent the hot sugar syrup from burning. A large heavy-based saucepan is essential, and to prevent the mixture from boiling over, the inside of the pan should be brushed with oil just above the level of the sugar syrup. Do not stir the mixture unless the recipe states that you should otherwise the toffee will crystallise.

The toffee should be allowed to boil very slowly indeed. It is a good idea to remove the pan from the heat just before the required temperature is reached to avoid overheating, leaving the thermometer in the syrup just to make certain. The mixture should be poured into the tins immediately and marked into squares or fingers with an oiled knife before the toffee is completely set.

Pulled toffees are fun to make and very attractive to look at. They can be cut into squares, oblongs or cushion shaped sweets using oiled scissors. The instructions for how to carry out this delightfully messy process are on page 86.

When set, toffees and caramels should be wiped carefully with kitchen paper towel to remove any oil and then wrapped individually in waxed papers.

Store toffees, caramels and brittles in an airtight tin, but eat them up quickly as they are inclined to go soft.

Golden toffee

450 g (1 lb) granulated sugar
50 g (2 oz) butter
10 ml (2 tsp) vinegar
about 225 g (8 oz) golden syrup
15 ml (1 tbsp) water

Butter a 20.5 × 15-cm (8 × 6-in) tin. Put all the ingredients in a heavy-based saucepan and boil quickly to 149°C (300°F) (hard crack stage). Pour into the tin and allow to cool. Mark into squares when almost set.
Makes about 700 g (1½ lb)

Honey caramels (*page 93*), Golden caramels (*page 92*), Chocolate caramels (*page 100*), Cream caramels (*page 91*), Walnut caramels (*page 93*) ▶

Creamy toffee

450 g (1 lb) light brown soft sugar
150 ml (¼ pint) milk
15 ml (1 level tbsp) golden syrup
50 g (2 oz) butter
1 small can condensed milk

Butter an 18 × 12.5-cm (7 × 5-in) tin. In a heavy-based saucepan, dissolve the sugar in the milk over a gentle heat, then add the syrup and butter. Bring to the boil and boil for 2–3 minutes before stirring in the condensed milk. Re-boil and heat to 116°C (240°F) (soft ball stage). Beat until creamy, then pour into the tin. Mark into squares and leave until set.
Makes about 700 g (1½ lb)

Everton toffee

450 g (1 lb) granulated sugar
150 ml (¼ pint) milk
30–45 ml (2–3 tbsp) double cream or evaporated milk
50 g (2 oz) butter, melted
pinch salt
pinch cream of tartar
few drops of lemon essence or other flavouring

Grease several shallow tins or a marble, enamel or wooden surface and caramel bars. Dissolve the sugar in the milk in a heavy-based saucepan, then boil to 121°C (250°F) (hard ball stage). Slowly add the cream or evaporated milk, stirring all the time, and boil to 132°C (270°F) (soft crack stage).

Take the pan off the heat and add the melted butter and the remaining ingredients. Mix well, then return to the heat and carefully boil to 140°C (285°F) (soft crack stage). Pour the toffee into the tins, cr into the caramel bars on the prepared surface.
Makes about 700 g (1½ lb)

Honeycomb toffee

450 g (1 lb) granulated sugar
300 ml (½ pint) water
60 ml (4 tbsp) vinegar
2.5 ml (½ level tsp) bicarbonate of soda, sifted

Butter a 30.5 × 10-cm (12 × 4-in) tin, or an 18-cm (7-in) square tin. Dissolve the sugar in the water and vinegar in a deep, heavy-based saucepan. Bring to boiling point and boil gently to 140°C (285°F) (soft crack stage).

Remove from the heat and add the bicarbonate of soda to the toffee. Mix thoroughly and pour into the prepared tin. Mark into squares or fingers before completely set.
Makes about 450 g (1 lb)

Plain and stripy Peppermint humbugs (*page 88*), Walnut molasses, Toffee humbugs (*page 90*), Barley sugar twists (*page 89*)

Hazelnut toffee

75 g (3 oz) shelled hazelnuts, blanched and chopped
450 g (1 lb) granulated sugar
25 g (1 oz) butter
10 ml (2 tsp) vinegar
150 ml ($\frac{1}{4}$ pint) water
pinch salt
5 ml (1 tsp) vanilla essence

Butter a 30.5 × 10-cm (12 × 4-in) tin or an 18-cm (7-in) square tin. Warm the nuts in the oven at 130°C (250°F) mark $\frac{1}{2}$. Put all the ingredients except the nuts and the essence into a 2.3-litre (4-pint) heavy-based saucepan and stir until dissolved. Boil the mixture to 149°C (300°F) (hard crack stage).

Add the vanilla essence to the toffee and pour half the toffee into the tin. Sprinkle the warmed nuts over the surface then pour over the remaining toffee. Mark into squares when almost set.
Makes about 550 g (1$\frac{1}{4}$ lb)

Helensburgh toffee

100 g (4 oz) butter
300 ml ($\frac{1}{2}$ pint) milk or water
900 g (2 lb) granulated sugar
1 large can condensed milk
7.5 ml (1$\frac{1}{2}$ tsp) vanilla essence

Butter a 20.5-cm (8-in) square tin. Melt the butter with the milk or water in a heavy-based saucepan. Add the sugar and, stirring gently, slowly bring to the boil. Boil until it reaches 116°C (240°F) (soft ball stage). Add the condensed milk, then re-boil to soft ball consistency, beating with a wooden spoon all the time.

Remove from the heat and let cool slightly. Add the essence, then beat with a wooden spoon for about 5 minutes until the mixture begins to grain. Quickly pour into the tin. Mark into squares or fingers before completely cold.
Makes about 1.1 kg (2$\frac{1}{2}$ lb)

Note More like fudge than toffee, this keeps for up to 2 weeks.

Caramelled almonds

200 g (7 oz) preserving sugar
10 ml (2 tsp) water
50 g (2 oz) split blanched almonds

Grease a 20.5 × 15-cm (8 × 6-in) tin. Dissolve the sugar in the water in a heavy-based saucepan and heat gently until it becomes a light coffee colour and reaches a temperature of 154°C (310°F) (hard crack stage). Take care not to let the caramel over-heat and burn. Stir in the almonds, pour into the tin and spread with a spoon until it is 0.5 cm ($\frac{1}{4}$ in) thick. When nearly set, mark into small squares. Wrap in waxed paper or cellophane when cold and store in an airtight tin.

Makes about 225 g (8 oz)

Note The almonds in this toffee do not keep crisp for any length of time – a good excuse for eating it up as quickly as possible.

Almond toffee squares

450 g (1 lb) demerara sugar
150 ml ($\frac{1}{4}$ pint) water
few drops of almond essence
75 g (3 oz) blanched almonds, halved

Grease a 20.5-cm (8-in) square tin. Put the sugar and water into a heavy-based saucepan and boil without stirring until a temperature of 154°C (310°F) (hard crack stage) is reached. The temperature must be watched carefully, as it rises rapidly and the flavour will be spoilt if it is allowed to go higher than this.

Add the almond essence. Spread the almonds on the tin and pour the toffee on to them to form a thin sheet. When sufficiently cool, mark into squares. Break up the toffee when cold.

Makes about 450 g (1 lb)

Brazil nut toffee

75 g (3 oz) shelled Brazil nuts
450 g (1 lb) granulated sugar
25 g (1 oz) butter
10 ml (2 tsp) vinegar
30 ml (2 tbsp) water
pinch salt
5 ml (1 tsp) vanilla essence

Grease a 20.5-cm (8-in) square tin. Toast the nuts for a few minutes, chop roughly and keep hot. In a heavy-based saucepan, gently heat all the ingredients except the nuts and essence, stirring until the sugar dissolves. Boil the toffee without stirring, until it reaches 149°C (300°F) (hard crack stage); add the essence.

Pour half of the boiling toffee mixture into the prepared tins. Sprinkle the hot nuts on top, then pour the remainder of the toffee over. When it is almost set, mark it into squares.
Makes about 450 g (1 lb)

Butterscotch

450 g (1 lb) demerara sugar
150 ml (¼ pint) water
50–75 g (2–3 oz) unsalted butter

Butter a 18 × 12.5-cm (7 × 5-in) tin. In a heavy-based saucepan, dissolve the sugar in the water over a low heat and boil to 138°C (280°F) (soft crack stage), brushing down the sides of the pan occasionally during the boiling with a brush dipped in cold water. Add the butter a little at a time and pour the mixture into the tin. Cut into pieces when almost set.
Makes about 450 g (1 lb)

Brushing down the sides of the pan to prevent crystals forming when boiling Butterscotch

Treacle toffee

450 g (1 lb) demerara sugar
150 ml ($\frac{1}{4}$ pint) water
1.25 ml ($\frac{1}{4}$ level tsp) cream of tartar
75 g (3 oz) butter
100 g (4 oz) black treacle
100 g (4 oz) golden syrup

Butter a 30.5 × 10-cm (12 × 4-in) tin. Dissolve the sugar in the water in a large heavy-based saucepan over a low heat. Add the remaining ingredients and bring to the boil. Boil to 132°C (270°F) (soft crack stage). Pour into the tin, cool for 5 minutes, then mark into squares and leave to set.
Makes about 800 g (1$\frac{3}{4}$ lb)

Brittles

Peanut brittle

350 g (12 oz) unsalted peanuts, chopped
400 g (14 oz) granulated sugar
175 g (6 oz) light brown soft sugar
175 g (6 oz) corn or golden syrup
150 ml ($\frac{1}{4}$ pint) water
50 g (2 oz) butter
1.25 ml ($\frac{1}{4}$ level tsp) bicarbonate of soda

Butter a 30.5 × 10-cm (12 × 4-in) tin. Warm the nuts in the oven at 130°C (265°F) mark $\frac{1}{2}$. In a large heavy-based saucepan gently heat the sugars, syrup and water until the sugar is dissolved. Add the butter and bring to the boil; boil very gently to 149°C (300°F) (hard crack stage). Add the bicarbonate of soda and warmed nuts. Pour the toffee slowly into the tin and mark into bars when almost set.
Makes about 1.1 kg (2$\frac{1}{2}$ lb)

Almond brittle

350 g (12 oz) preserving sugar
150 ml ($\frac{1}{4}$ pint) water
225 g (8 oz) golden syrup
10 ml (2 level tsp) powdered glucose
25 g (1 oz) butter
75 g (3 oz) blanched almonds, chopped and toasted
2.5 ml ($\frac{1}{2}$ tsp) lemon essence
7.5 ml (1$\frac{1}{2}$ level tsp) bicarbonate of soda

85

Oil a marble or enamel slab or wooden chopping board. Dissolve the sugar in the water with the golden syrup and the glucose, stirring occasionally. Boil to 149°C (300°F) (hard crack stage). Add the butter, almonds and essence and reheat to melt the butter.

Stir in the bicarbonate of soda and pour in a very thin sheet on to the prepared surface. Roll out immediately with an oiled rolling pin and break up when firm and brittle.
Makes about 700 g (1½ lb)

Coconut brittle   Make as for Almond brittle (*see above*) substituting 75–100 g (3–4 oz) desiccated or shredded coconut for the almonds.

Pulled toffees

Treating toffee mixtures by 'pulling' them produces the satiny, silvery look which is characteristic of such sweets as toffee humbugs. Work the toffee with a palette knife until it is cool enough to handle, but start the pulling as soon as you can touch it without burning your fingers because as the toffee cools, it also loses pliability. Oil your hands well and gather up the mixture. Twist it to make a rope about 51 cm (20 in) long, then fold the rope back on itself and pull and twist again, continuing to do this until the mixture is opaque, elastic and shiny.

For cushion-shaped sweets, finally pull out the toffee into an even roll about 2.5 cm (1 in) in diameter. Cut off 2.5-cm (1-in) pieces with oiled scissors, turning the roll so that each cut is at right angles to the previous one. Press each sweet lightly, uncut edges between finger and thumb, to make the corners 'pop up' to form cushions.

Other attractive effects can be achieved by combining pulled and unpulled toffee before cutting into shapes. To obtain a striped effect, pull half (or a smaller or larger proportion) of the toffee and keep the remainder warm meanwhile. Form both pulled and unpulled toffees into a roll, pressing them together, and pull out to the desired thickness, twisting the roll if liked, then cut into squares, cushions, oblongs, etc. (See the recipe for Peppermint humbugs on page 88.)

It is essential to handle the toffee quickly and efficiently when pulling, so the amateur would be wise to try simple toffee cushions before attempting striped effects, especially if working single-handed.

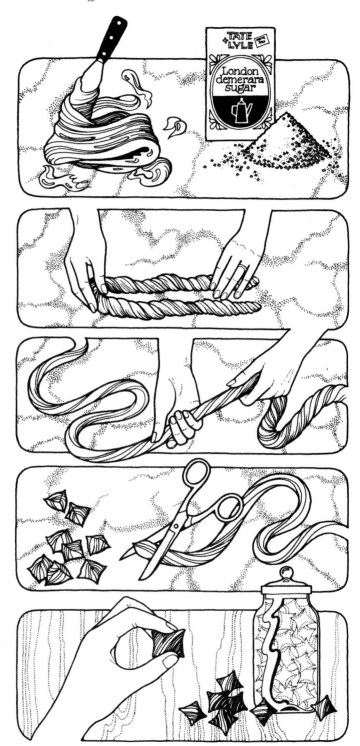

Pulling and shaping toffee. To make humbug shapes, twist the rope and cut with oiled scissors; press straight-cut pieces between finger and thumb to make toffee cushions

87

Peppermint humbugs

Illustrated in colour facing page 81

You really do need more than one pair of hands to make these stripy favourites, so enlist the help of a friend, or perhaps of a reasonably competent child. If liked, all of the toffee mixture can be pulled to make humbugs without stripes.

450 g (1 lb) granulated sugar
150 ml (¼ pint) water
1.25 ml (¼ level tsp) cream of tartar
15 ml (1 tbsp) golden syrup
few drops of peppermint essence
few drops of brown food colouring

Oil a marble or enamel slab or wooden chopping board. Dissolve the sugar in the water in a large heavy-based saucepan. Mix the cream of tartar with 15 ml (1 tbsp) water and add to the saucepan with the golden syrup. Bring the mixture gently to 154°C (310°F) (hard crack stage). Pour the syrup on to the slab and allow to cool a little.

Using oiled palette knives, fold the sides of the toffee into the centre and add a few drops of peppermint essence. When the mixture is cool enough to handle, cut off one-third and pull this until it is pale in colour, but still soft.

Meanwhile your helper should add a few drops of food colouring to the remaining toffee and gently form into a thick roll. Divide the pulled toffee into four ropes and press these against the sides of the thick darker rope. Pull out gently to the required thickness and twist. The larger the size of humbug you want, the thicker you will need to make the roll. Using oiled scissors cut into humbugs or cushions.

Makes about 450 g (1 lb)

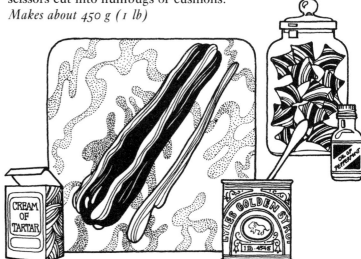

Sticking the 'stripes' on to Peppermint humbugs

Barley sugar walking sticks

450 g (1 lb) preserving sugar
150 ml ($\frac{1}{4}$ pint) water
thinly pared rind of $\frac{1}{2}$ a lemon
pinch cream of tartar
juice of $\frac{1}{2}$ a lemon

Oil a marble or enamel slab or wooden chopping board. Gently dissolve the sugar in the water in a heavy based saucepan, then add strips of lemon rind and the cream of tartar. Boil to 116°C (240°F) (soft ball stage), remove from the heat and add the lemon juice. Boil to 154°C (310°F) (hard crack stage).

Take the pan off the heat, remove the rind and pour the mixture on to the oiled slab. Cool it slightly, then fold the sides in to the middle using a palette knife and pull the toffee. Cut it into strips with oiled scissors and bend one end of each strip to make 'walking sticks'.

Makes about 450 g (1 lb)

Note Barley sugar quickly becomes sticky if it is left exposed to the air. Immediately it has become cold it should be stored in airtight jars.

Barley sugar twists

Illustrated in colour facing page 81

Replace 225 g (8 oz) of the sugar in the above recipe by 225 g (8 oz) powdered glucose and use a few drops of lemon essence instead of lemon juice. Put the sugar and water in a pan, dissolve slowly and add the glucose and lemon rind. Boil to 154°C (310°F) (caramel stage). Remove the rind, add the essence and pour the mixture on to the slab. When it is slightly cooled, fold sides to middle using a greased palette knife. Rub the fingers with oil and pull the mixture. Cut the pulled toffee into strips with oiled scissors and twist each strip.

Makes about 450 g (1 lb)

Almond toffee

450 g (1 lb) demerara sugar
150 ml ($\frac{1}{4}$ pint) water
25 g (1 oz) butter
2.5 ml ($\frac{1}{2}$ level tsp) cream of tartar
2–3 drops of acetic acid
30 ml (2 level tbsp) golden syrup
75 g (3 oz) blanched almonds, chopped

Oil a marble or enamel slab or wooden chopping board. Dissolve the sugar in the water in a heavy-based pan, cover and bring to the boil. Add the butter, cream of tartar, acetic acid and golden syrup. Cover again and boil for a few minutes.

Remove the lid and heat to 149°C (300°F) (hard crack stage). Pour on to the prepared surface, sprinkle with the nuts and turn the sides to the middle using a greased palette knife. When cold enough to handle, pull the toffee lightly with oiled fingers. When nearly set, cut into cushions or squares. Wrap in waxed paper or cellophane when cold and store in an airtight tin.
Makes about 550 g (1¼ lb)

Walnut molasses

Illustrated in colour facing page 81

450 g (1 lb) demerara sugar
150 ml (¼ pint) water
pinch cream of tartar
25 g (1 oz) butter
75 g (3 oz) shelled walnuts, chopped and toasted

Oil a marble or enamel slab or wooden chopping board. Dissolve the sugar in the water in a heavy-based saucepan and bring to the boil; add the cream of tartar and continue boiling to a temperature of 132°C (270°F) (soft crack stage). Add the butter in small pieces and boil to 138°C (280°F) (soft crack stage).

Pour the mixture on to the prepared surface and sprinkle with the nuts. Use an oiled palette knife to turn the sides into the centre until the mixture is cool enough to handle, then oil the fingers and pull the toffee out until it is about 1 cm (½ in) thick. Cut up and finish in the same way as for Toffee humbugs (*see below*).
Makes about 550 g (1¼ lb)

Toffee humbugs

Illustrated in colour facing page 81

450 g (1 lb) light brown soft sugar
50 g (2 oz) butter
150 ml (¼ pint) water
30 ml (2 level tbsp) golden syrup
2.5 ml (½ level tsp) cream of tartar
few drops of vanilla or almond essence, or 2.5 ml (½ level tsp) ground ginger, cinnamon or cloves to flavour

Oil a marble or enamel slab or wooden chopping board. Put everything except the cream of tartar and flavouring in a large heavy-based saucepan, dissolve the sugar and bring to the boil. Add the cream of tartar and boil to 143°C (290°F) (soft crack stage). Add the flavouring and pour the mixture on to the prepared surface. Leave the toffee until a skin has formed, then, using a flexible greased palette knife, turn the edges into the centre, continuing to work the toffee until it is cool and firm enough to handle. Scrape the toffee off the slab, form it into a rope and pull.

Quickly shape the toffee into a rope about 2 cm ($\frac{3}{4}$ in) in diameter and with oiled scissors cut off 2-cm ($\frac{3}{4}$-in) pieces, half twisting the toffee rope each time to give the correct humbug shape. Wrap each piece in waxed or cellophane paper and store the toffee in an airtight tin.

Makes about 450 g (1 lb)

Toffee cushions

Make as for Toffee humbugs (see opposite), but replace the brown sugar by white preserving sugar and include fruit flavourings and colourings as desired.

Walking sticks

Use the Toffee humbug recipe (see opposite), but cut into longer strips after pulling and bend one end of each to make 'walking sticks'.

Caramels

Cream caramels

Illustrated in colour facing page 80

225 g (8 oz) light brown soft sugar
30 ml (2 tbsp) water
100 g (4 oz) butter
few drops vanilla essence
45 ml (3 tbsp) single cream

Oil an 18 × 12.5-cm (7 × 5-in) tin or a 15-cm (6-in) square tin. Dissolve the sugar in the water in a heavy-based saucepan over a low heat. Add the butter, vanilla essence and cream and boil to 118–130°C (245–265°F) (hard ball stage). Pour the boiling caramel mixture into the prepared tin and when almost cold mark into squares with a caramel marker or a knife. Cut with a sharp knife and wrap neatly in waxed paper.

Makes about 350 g (12 oz)

Golden caramels

Illustrated in colour facing page 80

225 g (8 oz) granulated sugar
50 g (2 oz) powdered glucose
30 ml (2 level tbsp) golden syrup
60 ml (4 tbsp) water
60 ml (4 tbsp) milk
few drops of vanilla essence

Oil an 18 × 12.5-cm (7 × 5-in) tin. In a heavy-based saucepan, heat all the ingredients except the essence until the sugar is dissolved. Slowly heat the mixture to 124°C (255°F) (hard ball stage), stirring occasionally. Add a little essence, stir and pour the mixture into the tin. Mark with a knife and break into pieces when cold. Wrap individually, in waxed paper if possible.
Makes about 350 g (12 oz)

Russian toffee

450 g (1 lb) caster sugar
50 g (2 oz) butter
30 ml (2 level tbsp) golden syrup
1 large can condensed milk
5 ml (1 tsp) lemon juice

Grease a 30.5 × 10-cm (12 × 4-in) tin or an 18-cm (7-in) square tin. Heat the sugar, butter and syrup gently in a heavy-based saucepan stirring occasionally until the sugar has dissolved. Bring to the boil and add the condensed milk and lemon juice. Boil gently to 118°C (245°F) (soft ball stage) but do not stir.

Remove the pan from the heat and allow the bubbles to subside. Pour the toffee into the tin. Mark into squares with a buttered knife when half set. When set, divide and wrap.
Makes about 550 g (1¼ lb)

Soft vanilla caramels

450 g (1 lb) granulated sugar
150 ml (¼ pint) milk
120 ml (8 tbsp) liquid glucose
small can condensed milk
50 g (2 oz) butter
100 g (4 oz) desiccated coconut (optional)
few drops of vanilla essence

Grease a 30.5 × 10-cm (12 × 4-in) tin or an 18-cm (7-in) square tin. Heat the sugar and milk gently in a large heavy-based saucepan until the sugar is dissolved. Bring to the boil, add the liquid glucose and boil to 121°C (250°F) (hard ball stage). Now add the condensed milk slowly, stirring the boiling mixture

gently. Add the melted butter and the coconut. Boil up to 124°C (255°F) (hard ball stage), add the flavouring and pour into the prepared tin.
Makes about 700 g (1½ lb)

Honey caramels

Illustrated in colour facing page 80

75 g (3 oz) butter
150 g (5 oz) golden syrup
175 g (6 oz) honey
100 g (4 oz) walnuts, chopped
100 g (4 oz) dates, stoned and chopped

Grease a 15-cm (6-in) square tin. Melt the butter in a heavy-based saucepan, then add the syrup and honey and bring to the boil. Boil to 130°C (265°F) (hard ball stage). Remove from the heat and add the nuts and dates. Pour into the tin, leave until almost cold, then cut into squares and wrap in waxed paper.
Makes about 550 g (1¼ lb)

Walnut caramels

Illustrated in colour facing page 80

150 ml (¼ pint) milk
450 g (1 lb) preserving sugar
50 g (2 oz) golden syrup
25 g (1 oz) butter
50 g (2 oz) walnuts, chopped
5 ml (1 tsp) vanilla essence

Butter an 18 × 12.5-cm (7 × 5-in) tin. Heat the milk, sugar, syrup and butter slowly, in a heavy-based saucepan, stirring occasionally until the sugar has dissolved. Boil to 124°C (255°F) (hard ball stage), then stir in the warmed nuts and the essence. Stir until thick and pour into the tin. Cut when nearly cold.
Makes about 550 g (1¼ lb)

Tablets

Hazel tablet

900 g (2 lb) demerara sugar
300 ml (½ pint) water
5 ml (1 tsp) vanilla essence
75 g (3 oz) hazelnuts, chopped

93

Butter a 20.5-cm (8-in) square tin. In a heavy-based saucepan, quickly dissolve the sugar in the water. Bring it to the boil and continue boiling until a temperature of 118°C (245°F) (soft ball stage) is reached. Add the vanilla essence and nuts and continue boiling until it comes back up to temperature.

Allow the tablet to cool a little, then beat until it is well 'grained' but still liquid. Pour into the tin and cut into pieces when nearly set.

Makes about 1 kg (2¼ lb)

Ginger tablet

Follow the directions for Hazel tablet, but omit the vanilla essence and nuts and substitute 20 ml (4 level tsp) ground ginger. Do not re-boil after adding the ginger: just cool a little before beating.

Coconut tablet

300 ml (½ pint) milk and water mixed
25 g (1 oz) butter
900 g (2 lb) preserving sugar
2.5 ml (½ level tsp) cream of tartar
100 g (4 oz) desiccated coconut

Butter a 20.5-cm (8-in) square tin. In a heavy-based saucepan, gently heat the milk and water, butter and sugar, stirring frequently. Add the cream of tartar and stir occasionally. Boil to 116°C (240°F) (soft ball stage), then stir in the coconut. Cool a little and stir with either a wooden spoon or a spatula until creamy and white. Pour into the tin and cut into pieces when nearly set.

Makes about 1 kg (2¼ lb)

Fig tablet

Follow the recipe for Coconut tablet, substituting 100 g (4 oz) finely chopped figs for the coconut.

Nuts and nougats

Buttered nuts

450 g (1 lb) granulated sugar
75 g (3 oz) butter
30 ml (2 level tbsp) powdered glucose
150 ml (¼ pint) water
225 g (8 oz) shelled walnuts or almonds

Grease a marble or enamel slab or a baking sheet. Heat the sugar, butter, glucose and water in a heavy-based saucepan and bring to the boil, stirring until the sugar has dissolved. Heat to 149°C (300°F) (hard crack stage) then spoon small amounts on to the greased surface. Quickly put a halved nut on top of each and cover with a little more toffee. When set remove from the tin and wrap in waxed paper.
Makes about 800 g (1¾ lb)

Butternut drops

25 g (1 oz) blanched almonds
225 g (8 oz) demerara sugar
150 ml (¼ pint) water
pinch cream of tartar
50 g (2 oz) unsalted butter

Grease a baking sheet and position the nuts with 5-cm (2-in) spaces between them. Dissolve the sugar in the water in a heavy-based saucepan over a very low heat. Add the cream of tartar and butter, bring to the boil and boil gently to 138°C (280°F) (soft crack stage). Do not stir at this stage. Spoon a small amount of toffee mixture over each nut and allow to cool before lifting from the tin.
Makes about 225 g (8 oz)

Simple French nougat

rice paper
450 g (1 lb) granulated sugar
225 g (8 oz) powdered glucose
150 ml (¼ pint) water
2 egg whites
100 g (4 oz) blanched almonds, toasted and chopped
50 g (2 oz) angelica, chopped

Dampen the inside of a 20.5 × 15-cm (8 × 6-in) tin and line with rice paper. In a heavy-based saucepan, dissolve the sugar and glucose in the water over a gentle heat and boil to 132°C (270°F) (soft crack stage).

Beat the egg whites until stiff, then gradually beat in the syrup. As soon as the mixture begins to thicken, add the nuts and angelica, mix well, then pour into the tin. Cover with rice paper and press down with a heavy weight. Leave the nougat for at least 12 hours before cutting and wrapping in waxed paper.
Makes about 800 g (1¾ lb)

Nougat de Montélimar

rice paper
75 g (3 oz) honey
3 egg whites
50 g (2 oz) glacé cherries, chopped
25 g (1 oz) angelica, chopped
150 g (5 oz) blanched almonds, toasted and chopped
350 g (12 oz) granulated sugar
600 ml (1 pint) water
50 g (2 oz) powdered glucose
few drops of vanilla essence

Dampen a 30.5 × 10-cm (12 × 4-in) tin or an 18-cm (7-in) square tin and line it with rice paper. Melt the honey in a bowl over a pan of hot water, add the egg whites and beat until pale and thick.

Mix together the cherries, angelica and almonds. Dissolve the sugar in the water in a small heavy-based saucepan. Add the glucose and boil for about $4\frac{1}{2}$ minutes to 118–130°C (245–265°F) (hard ball stage). Add a few drops of vanilla essence.

Pour this syrup on to the honey mixture and continue beating over hot water until the mixture reaches 118–130°C (245-265°F) (hard ball stage). This may take 30–40 minutes, but is very important if the nougat is to set firmly. Add the fruit and nuts and put the mixture into the tin. Cover with more rice paper, put some weights on top and leave until quite cold. Cut into fingers and wrap in waxed paper.
Makes about 700 g ($1\frac{1}{2}$ lb)

Note This nougat will keep quite satisfactorily for 2 weeks.

Chocolate almond nougat

rice paper
450 g (1 lb) granulated sugar
150 ml ($\frac{1}{4}$ pint) water
100 g (4 oz) powdered glucose
50 g (2 oz) butter
2 egg whites, stiffly beaten
50 g (2 oz) cooking chocolate, melted
100 g (4 oz) blanched almonds, toasted and chopped

Dampen the inside of a 20.5 × 15-cm (8 × 6-in) tin and line with rice paper. Put the sugar in a heavy-based saucepan and dissolve it in the water over a low heat; add the glucose and butter and boil to 132°C (270°F) (soft crack stage).

Gradually add the syrup to the egg whites, beating all the time. Continue beating the mixture in a bowl over boiling water until it reaches 118–130°C (245–265°F) (hard ball stage). Add the chocolate and nuts, pour into the prepared tin and finish as above.
Makes about 700 g ($1\frac{1}{2}$ lb)

Chocolate Easter egg (*page 102*), Coconut haystacks (*page 101*), Chocolate fruit balls (*page 100*), Chocolate cups (*page 62*), Chocolate dipped fondants, caramels and peppermint creams (*page 103*) ▶

Chocolates to Cherish

*Simple, and more advanced,
coated, chocolates*

◀ Chocolate dipped fondants (*page 103*)

Everybody loves chocolates and a wide variety can be made successfully and impressively at home. There are two sorts of chocolate recipe in this chapter: first of all, fairly simple recipes in which chocolate is used to bind together other ingredients such as fruit and nuts; secondly, not so much recipes as ideas for combinations of centre, coating and decoration for making the more elaborate dipped chocolates.

Many of the fondants, marzipans, caramels, etc., for which we have given recipes elsewhere in this book make ideal centres for dipping in melted chocolate, and variety in shapes comes naturally with the different types of sweets being covered, for example round fondants, square toffees, oval nuts, etc. It is the finishing of the chocolates that puts on the style, and crystallised flowers, whole nuts and glacé fruits are just some of the decorations that can be used. The dipping forks themselves can be used to make a pattern, or else contrasting chocolate (plain on milk, milk on plain) can be piped in a pattern, using a small greaseproof paper icing bag fitted with a plain nozzle. See the colour photographs facing pages 96 and 97 for examples of dipped chocolates.

What kind of chocolate?

For some recipes, plain block chocolate, chocolate drops and Kake Brand give very good results. Couverture chocolate, which gives the best results when making dipped chocolates, is obtainable from wholesalers. We give addresses of stockists on page 125.

Chocolate is temperamental. When melting it, it should be broken into small pieces and placed in a bowl over a saucepan of

Melting chocolate in a bowl over a saucepan of hot water

cold water. Make sure that the base of the bowl does not touch the water and that it is wedged into the pan so that no steam escapes round the sides of the bowl. (Humidity spoils the texture and gloss of finished chocolates and dipping is best done on a warm, dry day when there is no other steamy cooking taking place.) Heat the water gently but don't allow it to boil – a glass bowl enables you to see any tell-tale bubbles. Remove the pan from the heat and stir the chocolate until it is completely melted. If it starts to harden again before you have finished dipping, simply reheat it gently in the same way.

Store chocolates in an airtight tin. According to the type of chocolate used, sweets will lose their gloss fairly quickly and long term storage is not recommended.

Chocolate squares

100 g (4 oz) cocoa powder
100 g (4 oz) drinking chocolate powder
100 g (4 oz) butter
60 ml (4 level tbsp) caster sugar
5 ml (1 tsp) vanilla essence

Grease an 18-cm (7-in) square tin. Mix the cocoa and chocolate powders in a basin. Melt the butter in a saucepan and heat it until bubbling, then remove the saucepan from the heat and add the sugar. Mix in the powders and beat the mixture well, then add the vanilla essence. Turn the mixture into the tin and when cold, cut into squares.
Makes about 350 g (12 oz)

Chocolate nut balls

100 g (4 oz) plain chocolate, grated
25 g (1 oz) shelled nuts, chopped
50 g (2 oz) icing sugar, sifted
few drops of vanilla essence
little single cream

Put most of the chocolate and the nuts and sugar in a basin, add a few drops of vanilla essence and enough cream to mix to a stiff paste. Shape into small balls and roll these in the remaining chocolate.
Makes about 225 g (8 oz)

Chocolate caramels

Illustrated in colour facing page 80

25 g (1 oz) butter
150 ml (¼ pint) condensed milk
225 g (8 oz) granulated sugar
120 ml (8 level tbsp) golden syrup
50 g (2 oz) cocoa
2.5 ml (½ tsp) vanilla essence
225 g (8 oz) plain chocolate, melted (optional)

Butter an 18 × 12.5-cm (7 × 5-in) tin. Melt the butter in a heavy-based saucepan and add the milk, sugar and syrup. Stir over a gentle heat until the sugar is dissolved. Bring to boiling point, add the cocoa and boil to 124°C (255°F) (hard ball stage). Add the essence, pour the mixture into the tin and mark into pieces before completely set. Once the caramels are set, they may if liked be dipped into plain chocolate.
Makes about 450 g (1 lb)

Chocolate fruit balls

Illustrated in colour facing page 96

100 g (4 oz) nuts
100 g (4 oz) seedless raisins
100 g (4 oz) sultanas
grated rind of 1 orange
3.75 ml (¾ tsp) almond essence
225 g (8 oz) plain chocolate, grated

Grease a baking sheet. Mix the nuts, raisins and sultanas and put through a mincing machine or chop very finely. Add the orange rind and almond essence and form into small balls. Set aside to dry for 24 hours.

The next day melt the chocolate in a bowl over hot water, then leave it over the water so that it does not solidify too rapidly. Dip each ball in the melted chocolate, place on the baking sheet and allow to set in a cold place.
Makes about 550 g (1¼ lb)

Chocolate raisin drops

175 g (6 oz) seedless raisins
175 g (6 oz) seedless raisins

Line a baking sheet with waxed paper. Melt the chocolate in a bowl over hot water then add the raisins, and stir until they are well coated and the mixture is slightly thickened. Drop in spoonfuls on to the baking sheet and place in the refrigerator or in a cool place to set.
Makes about 350 g (12 oz)

Rich chocolate cups

150 g (5 oz) couverture chocolate
100 g (4 oz) plain chocolate, grated
100 g (4 oz) icing sugar, sifted
little rum
few pistachio nuts, finely chopped

Melt the couverture chocolate in a bowl over hot water and brush it over the inside of about 16 small foil cases. Leave them to dry. Mix the grated chocolate and icing sugar in a bowl, with sufficient rum to form a stiff paste. Fill the cases with this mixture, then cover them with a little more melted couverture chocolate. When nearly set, sprinkle with a little finely chopped pistachio nut.
Makes about 16

Chocolate dates

450 g (1 lb) dessert dates
100 g (4 oz) plain chocolate, grated
15 ml (1 tbsp) boiling water
2.5 ml ($\frac{1}{2}$ tsp) vanilla essence
silver balls to decorate

Slit the dates lengthways so that the stones may be removed without breaking the fruit. Put the chocolate, boiling water and vanilla essence into a small saucepan and stir over a gentle heat until the chocolate melts, then stand the pan inside another saucepan of boiling water so that the chocolate does not solidify too rapidly.

Use a small teaspoon to open each date and fill it with the melted chocolate. Gently press the sides of the dates together and decorate with silver balls. Allow to set in a cold place.
Makes about 550 g ($1\frac{1}{4}$ lb)

Coconut haystacks

Illustrated in colour facing page 96

225 g (8 oz) milk chocolate
75–100 g (3–4 oz) desiccated coconut

Line a baking sheet with waxed paper. Melt the chocolate in a bowl over hot water, then add sufficient desiccated coconut to give a stiff, rocky consistency. Place in small rough heaps on the baking sheet and leave in a cool place to set.
Makes about 350 g (12 oz)

Chocolate-covered peanut clusters

100 g (4 oz) plain chocolate
175 g (6 oz) roasted peanuts

Line a baking sheet with waxed paper. Melt the chocolate in a bowl over hot water stirring all the time. Remove from the heat and add the roasted peanuts. Stir until these are completely covered with chocolate and the mixture is well blended. Drop from a teaspoon on to the baking sheet and leave in a cool place to set.

Makes about 225 g (8 oz)

Chocolate Easter eggs

Illustrated in colour facing page 96

Tin or plastic moulds are essential for making eggs; they are available in various sizes. Use good quality couverture chocolate and prepare it as for chocolate dipping (see page 98 and 99 for detailed instructions).

Rub out the inside of the moulds with kitchen paper towel, half fill with the chocolate and tilt so as to run the couverture to the edge of the mould and coat it evenly all round. Do this two or three times, then pour the surplus back into the chocolate pan. Run the finger round the edge of the mould to remove surplus chocolate and turn it domed side up on a cool flat surface. As the shells cool, they will contract slightly and may be removed by pressing gently at one end. The outer glazed surface caused by contact with the mould must not be handled more than can be helped. The shells can be joined by lightly touching the two halves on to a warm, flat tin, so that just sufficient chocolate melts to enable them to set firmly together.

Wrap the eggs in tinfoil, or decorate them with ribbon, sugar or chocolate piping and so on.

Crispy chocolates

225 g (8 oz) plain chocolate
15 g (½ oz) butter
2 large egg yolks, beaten
100 g (4 oz) blanched almonds, finely chopped

Break the chocolate into small pieces and melt in a bowl over hot water. Remove from the heat and leave to cool.

Stir in the butter and egg yolks, then return the bowl to the hot water and stir for 2 minutes. Stir in 50 g (2 oz) of the almonds and leave to cool.

Toast the remaining almonds under the grill until golden brown. Roll the chocolate mixture into about 16 small balls and toss in the almonds.

Makes about 225 g (8 oz)

Dipped chocolates

Illustrated in colour facing pages 96,97

These are perhaps the most 'professional' looking chocolates you will make at home. Ordinary block or Kake Brand chocolate will do, but dipping is a time-consuming operation and it is as well to help ensure good results by using couverture chocolate (see page 125 for stockists). Follow our instructions on page 99 for melting the chocolate and make sure it is at the correct temperature for dipping by tasting – it should feel slightly cool on the tongue. If the chocolate is too warm, it will dry cloudy and white; if too cool, it will coat the centres too quickly.

Many of the fondants, fudges, caramels, etc, for which we give recipes in this book make ideal centres for dipped chocolates. Allow your imagination free rein, but if you are a novice chocolate maker and feel you would like some guidance as to what goes with what, the table below gives some suggested combinations of centre, coating and decoration. Place the centres on a baking sheet and warm them slightly before you begin.

When the chocolate is ready, lower the centres into it one at a time using a dipping fork. Lift each centre out, shake off any surplus chocolate by knocking the fork gently against the edge of the basin and place the sweet on a baking sheet lined with waxed paper. While the chocolate is still soft, make a pattern by pressing the dipping fork lightly on the top and lifting it off again gently, or else press on a decoration or pipe the top of the sweet with a little contrasting chocolate. When the chocolates have dried thoroughly, put them into paper cases.

Centre	*Coating*	*Decoration*
Peppermint creams	Plain chocolate, completely or half dipped	Use dipping fork
Coffee fondants	Plain chocolate	Piped milk chocolate or almond half
Orange fondants	Plain chocolate	Candied orange peel
Lemon creams	Plain chocolate	Piece of crystallised lemon
Rose hip creams	Milk chocolate	Crystallised rose petal
Opera creams	Plain chocolate	Sliver of glacé cherry or candied angelica
Tangerine creams	Milk chocolate	Small piece of crystallised orange peel
Marzipan balls	Plain chocolate	
Marzipan walnuts	Plain chocolate	Walnut half

Centre	Coating	Decoration
Vanilla fudge	Plain chocolate	Walnut or almond half
Fruit and nut fudge	Milk chocolate	Piped plain chocolate
Coffee walnut fudge	Plain chocolate	Half walnut
Coconut fudge	Plain chocolate	Use dipping fork
Date fudge	Plain chocolate	Use dipping fork
Ginger fudge	Plain chocolate	Crystallised ginger
Tutti frutti fudge	Milk chocolate	Sliver of glacé cherry or candied angelica
Cream caramels	Milk chocolate	Piped plain chocolate
Soft vanilla creams	Plain chocolate	Almond half
Walnut caramels	Milk chocolate	Walnut half
Marzipan truffles	Plain chocolate	
Mocha truffles	Milk chocolate	
Rich chocolate rum truffles	Plain chocolate	
Whole Brazil nuts	Milk chocolate	
Whole large almonds	Plain chocolate	

Trifle with a Truffle

A selection of fruit, nut and liqueur-flavoured truffles

These mouthwateringly delicious little sweets are believed to have originated in France, and larger truffles were served as part of a selection of cakes and biscuits at teatime.

Although traditionally associated with Christmas in this country, smaller truffles make ideal after-dinner sweets. They are usually chocolate based with the addition of flavourings such as rum, brandy, coffee, fruit and nuts. When completely set, they are tossed in chocolate or cocoa powder, chocolate vermicelli, coconut or chopped nuts, or they can be dipped in plain or milk chocolate. Vermicelli are the little strands of chocolate that can be purchased from confectioners' and grocers' shops.

Most truffles keep in an airtight tin for up to two months: those containing fresh cream should be eaten up quickly.

Cherry truffles

100 g (4 oz) fresh or stale cake crumbs, finely grated
1 small orange
25 g (1 oz) glacé cherries, finely chopped
50 g (2 oz) caster sugar
25 g (1 oz) ground almonds
60 ml (4 level tbsp) apricot jam
5 ml (1 tsp) water
chocolate vermicelli (plain and milk)

Grate the orange rind finely and add to the crumbs in a bowl. Add the cherries, sugar and almonds and mix well.

Heat the jam and water together in a small saucepan until runny, then sieve it into the cake crumbs. Mix the jam and crumbs until evenly blended. Shape the mixture into small even-sized balls and place on waxed paper. Roll the truffles in vermicelli, leave to dry and put into paper cases.
Makes about 225 g (8 oz)

Almond truffles

100 g (4 oz) fresh or stale cake crumbs
100 g (4 oz) caster sugar
100 g (4 oz) ground almonds
little apricot jam, heated and sieved
little rum or sherry
chocolate vermicelli

Trifle with a Truffle

Crumble the cake finely and add the sugar, ground almonds and enough hot apricot jam to bind it and give a fairly sticky mixture. Add rum or sherry to taste.

Shape into small balls, dip them into the remaining jam and roll them in the chocolate vermicelli. Leave to harden, then put into paper cases.
Makes about 350 g (12 oz)

Chocolate rum truffles

Illustrated in colour facing page 57

225 g (8 oz) plain chocolate
15 ml (1 level tbsp) condensed milk
little rum
chocolate vermicelli

Melt the chocolate in a bowl over hot water, then add the milk and rum and beat well. Leave in a cool place until stiff enough to handle, then form into small balls and roll these in chocolate
Makes about 225 g (8 oz)

Rich chocolate rum truffles

225 g (8 oz) plain chocolate
2 egg yolks
25 g (1 oz) butter
10 ml (2 tsp) rum
10–20 ml (2–4 tsp) single cream
drinking chocolate powder

Melt the chocolate in a bowl over hot water, then add the egg yolks, butter, rum and cream. Stir until the mixture is thick enough to handle. Cool slightly, then form into balls and roll in chocolate powder. Leave until firm, then put in paper cases.
Makes about 225 g (8 oz)

Rich chocolate and brandy truffles

100 g (4 oz) plain chocolate
100 g (4 oz) unsalted butter
275 g (10 oz) icing sugar, sifted
little brandy
chocolate vermicelli

Melt the chocolate in a bowl over hot water then cream it with the butter and icing sugar and flavour with brandy. Form into small balls and roll these in chocolate vermicelli. Put into paper cases and allow to harden for a few hours.
Makes about 450 g (1 lb)

Chocolate orange liqueur truffles

Illustrated in colour facing page 57

Follow the recipe for Rich chocolate and brandy truffles (page 107), replacing the brandy with Grand Marnier and adding a little finely grated orange rind to the mixture. These truffles may be dipped in melted chocolate if liked.

Makes about 450 g (1 lb)

Chocolate cherry liqueur truffles

Follow the recipe for Rich chocolate and brandy truffles (page 107), replacing the brandy with Cherry Brandy and adding some chopped glacé cherries to the mixture.

Makes about 450 g (1 lb)

Mocha truffles

Illustrated in colour facing page 57

225 g (8 oz) plain chocolate
60 ml (4 level tbsp) condensed milk
few drops of coffee essence or strong black coffee
cocoa powder

Break the chocolate into small pieces and melt it in a bowl over hot water. Stir in the condensed milk and a few drops of coffee essence. Allow the mixture to cool slightly then form the mixture into small balls. Roll in cocoa powder and leave until set.

Makes about 225 g (8 oz)

Parisian truffles

Illustrated in colour facing page 57

350 g (12 oz) milk chocolate
75 ml (5 tbsp) single cream
2.5 ml ($\frac{1}{2}$ tsp) vanilla essence
chopped nuts

Line a medium-sized tin with waxed paper. Melt the chocolate in a bowl over hot water, and leave it to stand over the hot water for about 15 minutes. Scald the cream and let it stand until lukewarm.

Beat the chocolate until smooth, add the cream all at one time and beat again. Beat in the essence until well blended. Pour into the prepared tin and leave in a cold place until firm.

Form into small balls, and roll these in chopped nuts.

Makes about 350 g (12 oz)

Marzipan truffles

25 g (1 oz) chocolate
100 g (4 oz) marzipan
30 ml (2 level tbsp) nuts, ground or finely chopped
10 ml (2 tsp) vanilla essence
5 ml (1 tsp) sherry (optional)
drinking chocolate powder

Melt the chocolate in a bowl over hot water and knead it into the marzipan. Knead in the nuts, vanilla essence and sherry (if used), form into small balls and roll in chocolate powder.
Makes about 225 g (8 oz)

Chocolate nut truffles

100 g (4 oz) plain chocolate, finely grated
25 g (1 oz) shelled nuts, finely chopped
50 g (2 oz) icing sugar
1–2 drops of vanilla essence
little single cream
chocolate vermicelli

Put the chocolate, nuts and sugar into a bowl and add 1–2 drops of essence and sufficient cream to bind all the ingredients together. Form into small balls, roll them in chocolate vermicelli and put into paper cases when they are firm.
Makes about 225 g (8 oz)

Coffee truffles

Illustrated in colour facing page 57

225 g (8 oz) boiled fondant (see page 20)
10–15 ml (2–3 tsp) coffee essence or strong black coffee
10 ml (2 level tsp) condensed milk
90 ml (6 level tbsp) ground almonds
desiccated coconut or chopped nuts

Melt the fondant over hot water, then add the coffee essence and milk and remove from the heat. Stir until the mixture stiffens, add the ground almonds, form into balls and roll them in desiccated coconut or chopped nuts.
Makes about 350 g (12 oz)

Chocolate cream truffles

115 g (4½ oz) plain chocolate
60 ml (4 tbsp) double cream
10 ml (2 tsp) aromatic bitters
75 g (3 oz) cocoa powder
100 g (4 oz) icing sugar

Break the chocolate into small pieces and melt it in a bowl over hot water. Remove from the heat and leave to cool. Whisk the cream until stiff. Fold in the chocolate and aromatic bitters and leave until cold.

Sift 50 g (2 oz) of the cocoa powder and the icing sugar together. Beat into the chocolate mixture and shape into small balls. Toss the truffles in the remaining cocoa powder.
Makes about 225 g (8 oz)

Make Them Look Lovely

Presentation and packing:
simple containers to make;
renovating used tins and boxes;
some ideas for trimming

Good quality bought confectionery is always beautifully packed, one good reason being that if the outside looks attractive, the contents actually seem to taste better. This applies even more when you're making sweets or chocolates yourself to give as presents or to sell at fund-raising activities; crisp, pretty packaging sets off to best advantage those slightly irregularly shaped sweets that the inexperienced cook is likely to produce until he or she has developed the skill to make them look more professional.

Packaging isn't for looks alone, in any case – it's essential to protect the contents from being crushed or marked while in transit to the recipient or stall and also helps to keep them fresh and at the peak of perfection. So unless you're making a small batch for your family or guests to eat on the spot, it's best to store them in a tin overnight and then arrange them, individually wrapped if appropriate (see page 114) in their final packing.

Home-made packs can be simple and basic, smart and sophisticated, or even quite grand, according to whether it's a present for Granny or intended for sale to raise money for your favourite charity. Children love to help to make these containers, particularly if they've had a hand in producing the goodies. Most of the suggestions included here can safely be followed by ten-year-olds upwards, who will enjoy making up the boxes and other packs for which we give diagrams on pages 119–123. they'll also enjoy renovating used containers in some of the ways we've suggested. It's not a good idea, however, to let them loose with a spray can of silver paint as, apart from spraying everything in sight, nasty accidents can happen if a misdirected squirt lands in someone's eyes. But if you provide them with wrapping paper, cardboard, suitable glue and a stack of magazines from which to cut out decorative motifs, it should ensure a happy and relatively peaceful rainy Sunday afternoon.

Packing is just as enjoyable as making the sweets, so don't let the family have all the fun. You'll probably want to make the packs yourself in any case if the sweets are meant for sale and you are hoping to make them look a bit more professional. Tying ribbon bows, for instance, requires a neat-fingered skill that adults are more likely to have gained in the course of dressmaking. If on the other hand you're all fingers and thumbs when it

Top row Wedge-shaped carton, cracker, small cube box, bought box
Middle row Recycled tea tin, box, toffee tin, coffee tin
Bottom row Elliptical carton, 2 bought boxes, cone
(see pages 115–125 for diagrams or instructions) ▶

comes to gift wrapping, there is a wide range of well-designed boxes and ribbon bows to be found in department stores and good stationers. The only snag is that they add quite considerably to the cost of the ingredients for your confectionery.

There are in fact several approaches to packaging: the lazy way, buying ready-made packs and trimming them; the more enterprising way, to make them yourself, from scratch, as shown in our diagrams; and the 'recycling' method – perhaps the most fun and certainly the cheapest – when you make use of cartons, tins and other containers that you can find around the house, refurbish them and make them look fresh and pretty.

Equipment for packaging
If you're making, 'recycling' or adapting containers, you will need the following:

Scissors (for cutting paper and thin card)
Curved scissors (helpful for cutting out motifs, etc.)
Artist's scalpel, Stanley knife or other sharp knife (only if you are cutting heavier card; obviously not for children)
Metal ruler
Pointed knife, not too sharp (for scoring crease lines on card; younger children can use a ball point pen)
Pair of compasses (for circles and curves; young children can draw round glasses etc.)
Punch (for making holes through which to thread ribbon etc.)
Adhesive and small spatula (Cow Gum is easiest to handle)
Waxed paper (obtainable from good stationers or specialist suppliers, or use inner wrapping from cereal cartons)
Coloured card, thin to medium
  weight   (obtainable from
Metallic paper in, say, gold, silver, art shops)
  red and green
Wrapping paper (cheaper than 'art' paper: small, neat designs are easier for covering boxes and tins effectively)
Self-adhesive gift wrapping 'ribbon'
Cling film
Narrow satin ribbon
Narrow braid
Stick on transfers   (for trimming and
Double-sided adhesive tape   decorating)
Wallpaper scraps, old magazines

You will also need a firm wooden surface for working on such as a pastry board or back of an old wooden tray.

Before you decide how to pack your confectionery, however, you will need to prepare it.

Preparing confectionery for packaging

Some sweets need to be individually wrapped before being packed. Use cellophane, cling film, aluminium foil or waxed paper (obtainable from good stationers) to wrap boiled sweets, toffees, caramels and nougats. Square and oblong sweets can be done up in neat little parcels. Alternatively, the wrapping can be twisted at each end in opposite directions; other shapes such as rounds, cushion humbugs, etc., can be wrapped in the same simple way.

Sweets that are to be displayed may be given an over-wrapping of metallic paper, stocked by stationers and artists' suppliers, in gold, silver or various other colours. The choice of colours is a matter of taste but while giving brightness to a box of sweets, they must be used with restraint. Colours that are too bright may cheapen the appearance of the box and indeed, of the sweets.

Keep the wrapped sweets in a shallow tin until the containers are ready to be packed. Confectionery that is not to be wrapped individually needs to be placed singly in sweet cases – these are obtainable in brown for chocolates; patterned, and in gold and silver foil. Cased sweets should also be stored in a shallow tin until packed.

How to pack sweets and other confectionery

The type of sweet and the most suitable container for this type should be given careful consideration. Toffees, caramels and most hard sweets can be packed in cones, crackers, dolly bags, cellophane wrap-over bags, etc. Fondants, creams and jellies really need the protection of a rigid container.

Sweets shouldn't be haphazardly packed, but arranged for maximum effectiveness of juxtaposition of colour, shapes and type. They must also be packed closely together to prevent them from moving.

Start by lining the box with waxed or greaseproof paper. Dark waxed paper can be purchased from specialist suppliers and should be used if chocolates are being packed as any marks will not show. Every single item needs to be either individually wrapped or placed in a case and arranged in rows in the box. The rows should be separated with double thickness greaseproof or waxed paper. If they are to be layered a piece of cardboard or waxed paper should be placed between the layers.

When the box is filled it should be made as airtight as possible. If the box is lidded, a piece of padded or corrugated paper helps to protect the chocolates. If the box or other container does not have a lid, it should be covered with a piece of cling film or cellophane pulled tautly across the surface.

PACKAGING

1. Bought boxes and other containers

Many gift shops, some stationers and specialist firms (see page 125) stock these in a variety of shapes, sizes and colours, mostly rather bright but including sophisticated browns and blacks. The type sold flat and ready creased are usually easy to assemble but will need lining with waxed paper or foil unless the sweets to be put into them are wrapped. They don't really need any other trimming than a length of gold thread or narrow satin ribbon to tie them. Being professionally designed, they certainly make a very effective presentation for your sweets but, apart from the added cost, they are mostly too deep for any type of confectionery that will suffer from being packed one on top of another, unless the layers are separated with pieces of card. Brightly coloured miniature carrier bags are also available – though pretty and inexpensive, they give little or no protection.

Empty chocolate boxes are also obtainable at specialist shops but these do add considerably to one's outlay – as do the small baskets that are particularly suitable for Easter eggs.

2. Recycling used containers

You need only look round the house to see all sorts of used cartons, boxes, tins and so on that can be recycled and made to look brand new and completely different. When searching for boxes or other packs, don't be tempted to use any that have held soap or other perfumed contents (if you like a particular pack and can't use it for this reason, you may be able to open it out and use it as a pattern to make your own). Any box that you plan to re-use needs a fresh lining of waxed paper; alternatively, for a really attractive display, line it with a paper doyley and fold the opposite sides over the top of the sweets.

A carton of a suitable shape and size can often be recycled by opening it out flat, covering the inner side with a pretty wrapping paper and reassembling it inside out, as follows:

Recycling a carton

A small carton that has held tea sachets, after-dinner mints, etc, is ideal for home-made sweets. An example of just such a recycled box is shown in the colour illustration facing page 112.

Open it out carefully, so you don't tear the tabbed edge where it was previously stuck, and lay it out flat. Dab a very little adhesive all over the plain side and place a sheet of wrapping paper on top, smoothing out gently. Trim the paper back accurately to the edges of the carton, refold along the original creases and stick the tabbed edges as before. Gum a matching or contrasting piece of paper on the inside of the lid, which will show when the box is open. The sweets can nestle on a matching soft paper napkin or paper doyley.

This is the easiest and quickest way to make a professional looking box because the crease lines are already formed for you.

Recycling used tins

Often a tin that has held toffee, humbugs, etc., is still perfectly sound but a bit tired looking. Other tins that are suitable for refurbishing are those that have held coffee, cocoa, drinking chocolate, syrup, or dried milk, since these all have self-sealing lids that help to keep the sweets airtight. All tins should be thoroughly cleaned and dried before decorating and trimming. A selection of recycled tins are shown in the colour illustration facing page 112.

Paint the outside by spraying, having masked the inside with crumpled paper to prevent the paint going inside, or use acrylic paint applied with a brush. Several coats may be necessary to cover the surface evenly. Patterns can be stencilled or hand painted on to the side. Trim with braid, transfer motifs, etc., which can be applied with glue.

Alternatively, cover the tins with pretty wrapping paper.

To paper a round tin e.g. a coffee tin, measure the circumference (distance round) and height, accurately. Cut a strip of the wrapping paper the same length as the circumference, plus a centimetre for overlap, making the width the height of the tin. Glue the reverse side of the paper very lightly – too much and it will wrinkle – and then position the tin on the glued strip of paper and roll it until it is smoothly and evenly covered. Cut out a circle of the paper or contrasting card to fit the lid and glue this in place. The top and bottom edge can be finished, if you like, with a length of narrow ribbon or braid.

To paper a shallow rectangular metal box : starting with the lid, cut out a piece of wrapping paper slightly bigger than the combined measurements of the top and sides, both length and breadth (so as to allow for turning the paper under to the inside, for a neat finish). If the paper has a pronounced pattern, take care to position motifs effectively. Glue the area of the paper that is to cover the top of the lid very lightly, apply it to the lid, smooth out, and then slash the paper overlapping at the corners back to the corners of the lid. Paste the overlapping edges of the paper and turn under the sides of the lid, trimming if necessary. The box itself, provided it is shallow enough, can be covered in the same simple way, with a single piece of paper.

3. Other round-the-house ideas for containers

These ideas are not so much recycling as adapting containers originally designed for other purposes to make them suitable for holding sweets. First, freezer packs of various types are ideal.

Wax containers

These can be bought from most stationers and come in varying shapes and sizes, some more suitable than others for packing sweets. The best shapes are shallow containers for one or two layers; they usually have fold-over lids that help to keep the sweets airtight and need only to have two holes punched through so that you can thread the holes with ribbon.

If the containers you happen to have are of the taller type, you can easily make them shallower by cutting them down to size, literally, with a pair of scissors. Cut across two opposite sides at the desired height. Cut down the other sides to the bottom, then across the bottom. Remove the base (which will be attached to the two pieces of the sides that you cut away) and you are left with two flaps that can be folded over to form a new base. Stick the overlapping flaps together.

Wax containers can be trimmed with self-adhesive ribbons, braids and applied decorative motifs cut from wallpaper or magazines. Even if you find it hard to tie ordinary ribbon to make a bow that 'sits' well, it's easy to make either bows or pompom shapes with these stick-to-themselves ribbons. They're also a lot less expensive than draper's ribbon.

Foil containers

Shallow flan or baking tin foil containers make very effective packaging. These display the contents well and should be covered with cling film or Cellophane to protect the sweets. This is a particularly attractive way to display sweets that are to be sold because one can see the contents. The containers look more attractive if they are edged with a decorative ribbon or braid or lined with a paper doyley. They need to be finished with a ribbon or bow to make them really appealing. A small posy of violets or primroses placed on top are an attractive way to finish them.

Polystyrene and other disposable containers

The shallow square or oblong containers in which apples, tomatoes, etc., are sold in supermarkets make excellent little trays for sweets. Mask them with a pretty paper doyley. Paper plates can be treated in the same way – stick a circle of pink or blue tissue paper to the plate and fix a silver or gold paper doyley on top. Shallow plastic bowls as sold for picnics and parties are also suitable.

Jars, glasses, etc

Glass jars with stoppers or even the ordinary screw top kind can be used for sweets that don't crush easily. Cover with strips of paper or cut out motifs and decorate with a ribbon bow. Odd mugs, glasses and cups and saucers look pretty filled with sweets and covered with cling film.

4. Making your own boxes and other types of pack

The simplest packs to make, using decorative paper of one kind or another, are dolly bags, cones and crackers.

Dolly bags

Make these from crepe or tissue paper, cellophane or any decorative paper that is not too stiff. To protect the sweets a lining of waxed or greaseproof paper should be used. Cut equal-sized circles of decorative and greaseproof paper. Lay the decorative paper pattern side down and the greaseproof circle on top. With a darning needle and gold or silver thread, make a line of running stitches through both thicknesses about 1 cm ($\frac{1}{2}$ in) from the edge. Pull the thread gently to form a drawstring. A round of card at the bottom of the bag will help protect sweets.

Cones (see colour illustration facing page 112)

Cones make simple and effective containers for sweets. They may be varied in size according to the quantity of sweets you want them to contain. To make, cut out equal sized squares of greaseproof and decorative papers. Holding the opposite two corners, roll them together, towards you, so that they overlap to form a cone. Secure the overlapping corners above, and the point below, with staples or glue. The triangular top can be folded over the sweets to protect them.

Crackers (see colour illustration facing page 112)

These make attractive containers for sweets and may be made of various sizes – a small cracker is suitable for packing one or two truffles, while a larger cracker will hold a selection of sweets.

1. Cut out equal sized rectangular pieces of greaseproof or waxed paper and crepe, cellophane or decorative paper.

2. Cut out a piece of card the same width as the paper, but only one third its length. Place the outer paper, pattern side down, the greaseproof paper on top and the card on top of that so that an equal length of the papers extends at each end.

3. Carefully roll the papers together, around the piece of card, to form a cylinder. Twist one end of the cracker about 5 cm (2 in) from the end. Fill the cracker with sweets and then twist the other end. The crackers may be decorated with ribbons, bows or decorative motifs, and the ends snipped in zig-zag points to make an attractive finish.

Handling card

To make your own boxes (and other packs using card) success-fully, you have to acquire a little skill in scoring the card accurately along lines that are to be creased and bent during the making. Work on a hard flat wooden surface that won't matter if your first attempt at scoring goes slightly awry.

Mark the line to be scored with pencil, place a metal ruler on the line and then lightly draw the point of a sharp knife, Stanley knife or artist's scalpel along the line, against the ruler. An adult should undertake this part of the job if a child is going to complete the box. Trial and error will show you how deeply to cut – too shallow and you won't be able to bend the card along the line, too deep and the card will fall apart.

For the card, you have the alternatives of buying coloured card or white card which you will need to cover. If you're not sure what thickness of card to use, your local art shop will probably be able to advise you at the time of purchase. Children too young to be trusted with a sharp knife can work with thin card which can be scored with a ball point pen or sharp, hard pencil.

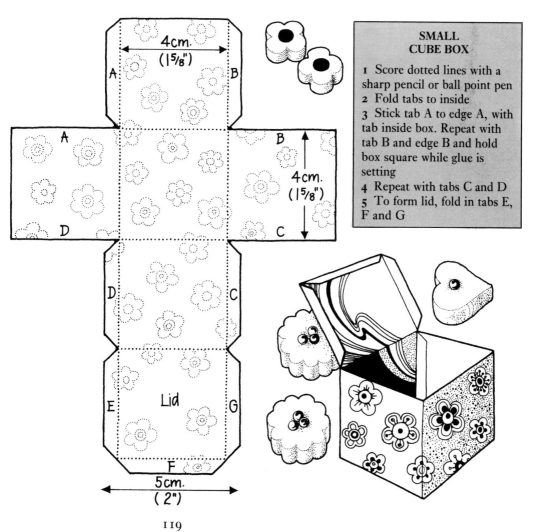

4cm.
(1⁵⁄₈")

4cm.
(1⁵⁄₈")

A   B

A   B

D   C

D   C

E   Lid   G

F

5cm.
(2")

SMALL CUBE BOX

1 Score dotted lines with a sharp pencil or ball point pen
2 Fold tabs to inside
3 Stick tab A to edge A, with tab inside box. Repeat with tab B and edge B and hold box square while glue is setting
4 Repeat with tabs C and D
5 To form lid, fold in tabs E, F and G

Small cube box (see diagram on page 119, and colour illustration facing page 112)
Use lightweight coloured card. For a small cube, follow the measurements indicated in the diagram; a larger one can be made to whatever size you think fit provided you remember that the squares must be equal. As you don't need a Stanley knife or scalpel for this box, only a pair of scissors, it is one that children can make without supervision. Draw out the shape accurately and cut out.

1. Score along all dotted lines with a sharp hard pencil or ball point pen.
2. Fold tabs to inside.
3. Stick tab A to edge A, with tab inside box. Repeat with tab B to edge B, with tab inside. Hold the box square while glue is setting.
4. Repeat with tabs C and D.
5. To form lid, fold in tabs E, F, G.

Wedge shaped carton (see diagram opposite and colour illustration facing page 112. Use lightweight coloured card. The dimensions given make a convenient size for a small quantity of sweets; the pack is 11 cm ($4\frac{3}{8}$ in) high and 10 cm (4 in) wide, 4 cm ($1\frac{1}{2}$ in) deep at the base. A scalpel or Stanley knife is needed to cut the slots. Draw and cut out shape.

1. Cut the four slots 2.3 mm ($\frac{1}{8}$ in) wide and 2 cm ($\frac{3}{4}$ in) long. Punch holes.
2. Score along all dotted lines and fold them all inwards.
3. Fold flap A into side 1. Repeat with flap B.
4. Fold flap C into side 2. Repeat, folding flap D.
5. Fold tongue E inwards on to base (3). Repeat with tongue F.
6. Open out flaps and tongues so card lies flat. Bring both sides together to match punched holes. Fold in flaps A, B, C, and D.
7. Tuck in tongues E and F through both slots.
8. Thread ribbon through punched holes.

Elliptical carton (see diagram on page 122, and colour illustration facing page 112). Use lightweight card. With its semicircular ends and curved front and back, this is a neat pack, measuring 15 cm (6 in) by 9 cm ($3\frac{1}{2}$ in), suitable for a small quantity of rather special sweets. A child old enough to be trusted with a pair of compasses (about seven upwards) can safely make this, though he may need help with the folding. Draw and cut out shape.

1. Score along all dotted lines. Use a compass point to score semicircular lines.
2. Stick tab A to face A.
3. Fold in ends so that semi-circles B are innermost. Trim lengthways with a piece of ribbon or gold thread.

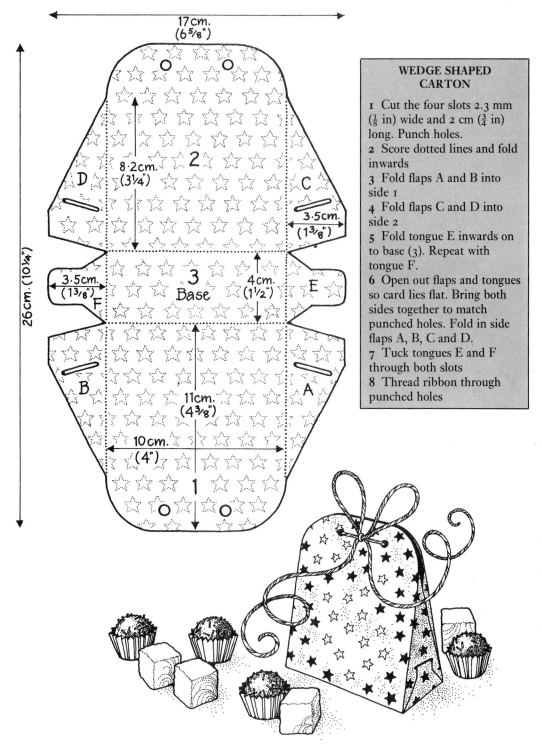

17cm.
(6⅝")

8·2cm.
(3¼")

D

2

C

3·5cm.
(1⅜")

26cm. (10¼")

3·5cm.
(1⅜")

3
Base

4cm.
(1½")

E

F

B

A

11cm.
(4⅜")

10cm.
(4")

1

**WEDGE SHAPED
CARTON**

1 Cut the four slots 2.3 mm
(⅛ in) wide and 2 cm (¾ in)
long. Punch holes.
2 Score dotted lines and fold
inwards
3 Fold flaps A and B into
side 1
4 Fold flaps C and D into
side 2
5 Fold tongue E inwards on
to base (3). Repeat with
tongue F.
6 Open out flaps and tongues
so card lies flat. Bring both
sides together to match
punched holes. Fold in side
flaps A, B, C and D.
7 Tuck tongues E and F
through both slots
8 Thread ribbon through
punched holes

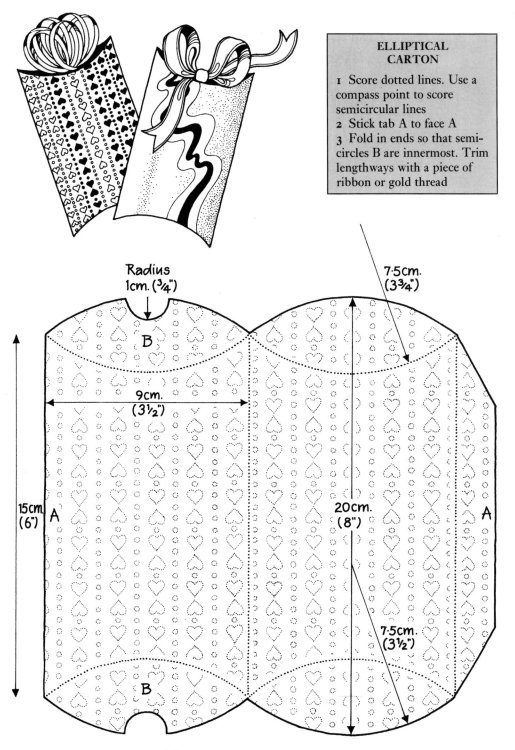

ELLIPTICAL CARTON

1 Score dotted lines. Use a compass point to score semicircular lines
2 Stick tab A to face A
3 Fold in ends so that semi-circles B are innermost. Trim lengthways with a piece of ribbon or gold thread

Radius 1cm. (¾")

7·5cm. (3¾")

B

9cm. (3½")

15cm (6")

A

20cm. (8")

A

7·5cm. (3½")

B

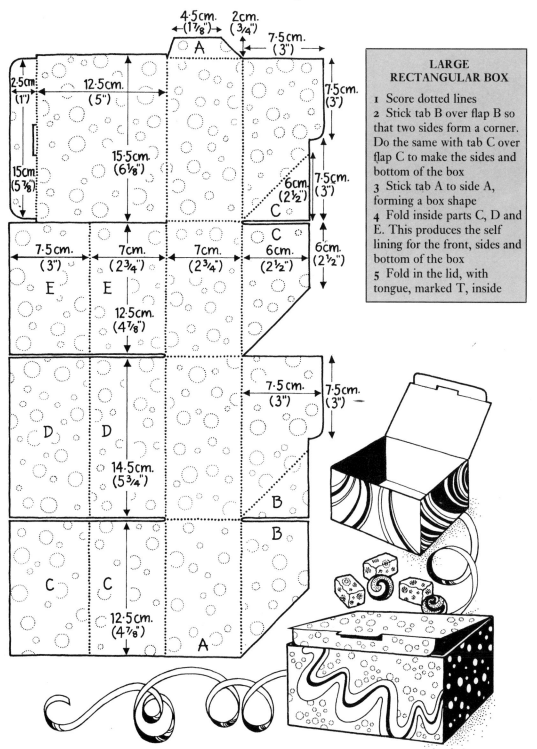

4.5 cm. (1⅞") 2 cm. (¾") 7.5 cm. (3")

A

2.5 cm. (1") 12.5 cm. (5") 7.5 cm. (3")

15 cm. (5⅞") 15.5 cm. (6⅛") 6 cm. (2½") 7.5 cm. (3")

C

7.5 cm. (3") 7 cm. (2¾") 7 cm. (2¾") 6 cm. (2½") 6 cm. (2½")

C

E E

12.5 cm. (4⅞")

D D

14.5 cm. (5¾")

7.5 cm. (3") 7.5 cm. (3")

B

C C

B

12.5 cm. (4⅞")

A

LARGE RECTANGULAR BOX

1 Score dotted lines
2 Stick tab B over flap B so that two sides form a corner. Do the same with tab C over flap C to make the sides and bottom of the box
3 Stick tab A to side A, forming a box shape
4 Fold inside parts C, D and E. This produces the self lining for the front, sides and bottom of the box
5 Fold in the lid, with tongue, marked T, inside

Large rectangular box (see diagram on page 123)
Use light or medium weight coloured card. The dimensions given make a strong, self-lined box, 15.5 cm (6⅛ in) across, 12.5 cm (4⅞ in) deep and 7 cm (2⅞ in) high. The design is slightly more complicated but you end up with a handsome box of suitable shape and size for chocolates or other confectionery needing the protection of a firm container. Draw and cut out, making the four grooves as accurately as possible.

1. Score along all dotted lines.
2. Stick tab B over flap B so that two sides form a corner. Do the same with tab C over flap C. This produces the sides and bottom of the box.
3. Stick tab A to side A, forming a box shape.
4. Fold inside parts C, D and E. This produces the self lining for the front, sides and bottom of the box.
5. Fold in the lid, with tongue marked T inside.

Trimming

The right trimming gives the finishing touch to the container, whether ready made, recycled, adapted or entirely home-made. We've given a number of ideas throughout this chapter. Apart from stationers and haberdashery departments, it's well worth trying specialist firms who sell braid, ribbon, sequins, motifs and other trimmings for stage costume, because they are likely to have a far wider range than the ordinary haberdashery counter.

Use rubber solution gum to stick ribbon, etc. Double sided adhesive transparent tape is also handy for making bows, rosettes, etc., though satin ribbon undoubtedly gives a better quality finish.

As with most things, simple is best, so don't make the trimming over-fussy or too bright, or it will make for an amateurish and cheap-looking result. Here are two simple trimmings.

Single bow (see diagram below)
The easiest way to make a bow, using self-adhesive ribbon. Take a short piece of ribbon, loop one end to the centre, having dampened it, and loop the other, also dampened, to the centre on top. Cut a short piece and wrap it round the middle of the bow, concealing both cut ends; dampen and secure in place.

Single bow

Multiple bow

Multiple bow (see diagram above)
This is made by making two bows, dampening and sticking one across the top of the other, and repeating the process until you have six pairs of bows. You then join these pairs together, dampening and sticking them one by one and joining them together diagonally. For a bow about 11.5 cm (4½ in) across, cut a dozen lengths of self-adhesive ribbon 5.6 cm (10 in) long and proceed as described.

USEFUL ADDRESSES

The following firms supply equipment, special ingredients or packaging materials of particular interest to anyone making confectionery at home.

Equipment

Leon Jaeggi & Sons Ltd.,	Elizabeth David,	David Mellor,
232 Tottenham Court Road,	46 Bourne Street,	4 Sloane Square,
London W.1	London S.W.1	London S.W.1
01-580 1957	01-730 3123	01-730 4259

Ingredients
The United Yeast Co. Ltd.,
Crown House,
Morden,
Surrey
01-542 6655

Packaging
Sweet cases, foil and waxed containers, self-adhesive ribbon, etc., are obtainable from most good stationers. Flat and made-up boxes and many other types of containers are obtainable from:

Paperchase Products Ltd.,	Selfridges,	John Lewis,
216 Tottenham Court Road,	Oxford Street,	Oxford Street,
London W.1	London W.1	London W.1
01-637 1121	01-629 1234	01-629 7711

Index

Index